REA

FRIEND<

OF ACPL

S0-BSF-812

THE
STARVING
FAMILY

Caregiving
Mothers and
Fathers Share
Their Eating
Disorder Wisdom

CHAMPION PRESS, LTD.
FREDONIA, WISCONSIN
Copyright © 2005 Cheryl Dellasega

ISBN: 1-932783-14-8
LCCN: 2004113157

MANUFACTURED IN THE UNITED STATES OF AMERICA

10 9 8 7 6 5 4 3 2 1

THE STARVING FAMILY

Caregiving Mothers and Fathers Share Their Eating Disorder Wisdom

Cheryl Dellasega, Ph.D.

CHAMPION PRESS LTD.

All of the author's proceeds from the sales of this book will be donated to the Eating Disorder Program at Penn State. For more information visit
http://www.hmc.psu.edu/eatingdisorders/

Acknowledgements

I wish to express deep gratitude to the many parent "coauthors" who shared their stories and wisdom, and to Lisa, Robin, and Benny for their expert reviews of the manuscript that resulted. My husband Paul provided incredible support in ways big and little that helped me persevere, and his legal advice came from the place in his heart that understands how parents feel. Brook Noel, the quintessential "can-do" girl and publisher extraordinare, believed in this concept from the very first email and dedicated herself to creating a book that will reach many. Finally, to the One who nurtures us all, thank you for somehow inspiring passion from pain.

Additional Support:

The Starving Family Companion Workbook offers worksheets to aide in the recordkeeping and support of those who care for children with eating disorders.

Published by Champion Press, Ltd. (2005)
ISBN: 1-932783-38-5

www.starvingfamily.com
The Starving Family website offers a supportive forum for caregivers to learn and communicate with one another.

Contents

FOREWORD
BY KITTY WESTIN

I love being a mother. I have always loved being able to comfort my children with a kiss, a kind word, or a gentle touch. Some of my fondest memories revolve around being available to them when they hurt themselves, felt ill, or needed someone to "kiss it and make it all better." For 20 years I had been able to help my daughter Anna and able to nurse her back to health from the stomach flu, bronchitis, or an ear infection. I knew when to take her to the doctor and get medicine; I knew my role, and I was confident that I was an important part of her recovery. Most importantly, I knew without a doubt that the best medicine was my time, attention, and love.

When Anna was diagnosed with anorexia I was woefully unprepared for what life would be like from then on. It seemed like overnight my skills as a mother, caregiver, and gentle healer were no longer valued. It was so difficult to get information. I often felt confused and isolated. Support for myself and my family was surprisingly hard to find. I felt alone and, for the first time as a mother, helpless and powerless. It did not take long for me to understand that we were basically on our own to learn about the disease. Both my husband and I felt angry, frustrated, and lost.

I don't think there are many words more frightening to a parent than: "Your child has an eating disorder." These words should be followed immediately by "... and here is a list of support groups, other parents who are willing to talk with you about their experience, educational materials, and organizations that may be helpful to you, your child, and your family." What comfort those words would have offered when Anna was first diagnosed with anorexia. Sadly, we did not hear them.

It is never easy caring for an ill child; it takes an incredible amount of time and energy, often at the expense of things like jobs, other children, and social activities. The "cost" to the family is enormous. It continues to astonish me that there is so little support when families are most vulnerable. This truly does create *starving families* who are confused, frightened, and lonely; families who desperately want to help and would do anything to save their child but don't know how.

In spite of all of our efforts, our daughter Anna died of anorexia on February 17, 2000. In those first horrific days and weeks our family somehow found ways to support each other. We received an enormous amount of care from our friends and the community.

We made the decision to find a way to transform our grief and rage into something positive and use Anna's story to help others. Because we had experienced it first hand we understood the issues families face including lack of support, battles with insurance companies, limited access to information, and lack of advocates. We set out to change this and within days of Anna's death we founded the Anna Westin Foundation. Four years later we are proud of what the foundation has accomplished. Our family continues to support each other and we have shared our story with millions through the media, public speaking, and advocacy efforts.

When I heard that a book was being written using the stories of families who had experienced caring for a child with an eating disorder I was thrilled. It makes sense to me that these parent "experts" are able to offer helpful and pertinent information to those in similar situations. Thank you to the many courageous families who were willing to share their experiences with Ms. Dellasega. Because of their generosity, other families will now have a guide and the opportunity to hear the voice of experience; to read honest accounts of the triumphs and trials, of victory and defeat and of the joys and sorrows associated with caring for a child with an eating disorder. As a result readers may feel less isolated, afraid, and frustrated. It is my wish that the voices of the families included in this book will offer hope and help to others and, in the end, give readers a voice of their own. I came across the following in Anna's journal. She wrote these words shortly before she died and I share them with you hoping that they will inspire you as they did me:

"May all your love, your joy and pain, all your fears and desires lead you to your own promises, may your dreaming never end and your voice never die."
Anna Westin (1999)

Kitty Westin
The Anna Westin Foundation
112329 Chatfield Court
Chaska, MN 55318
www.annawestinfoundation.org

4 ... THE STARVING FAMILY

INTRODUCTION
᚛ᚑᚌ

I know more about eating disorders than I want to — not by virtue of formal education, clinical experience, or sophisticated research. My "schooling" has come from those around me.

Periodically, members of my family have struggled with anorexia and bulimia, plunging all of us into a state of crisis and supporting the genetic theory of causation. Several of my close friends have been stricken with these diseases and during a particularly unhappy period in my life, I confronted anorexia. Most dramatically, my only daughter has battled anorexia and bulimia for several years, winding her way through so many treatment programs, therapists, and medications we've lost track of the details.

I still have lots of unanswered questions, and so much left to learn that it will be a lifelong process. Not long ago, I asked a psychiatrist who had treated my daughter if he had any insights on what might lead her to recover. He was silent after hearing my question, and then said:

"Mrs. Dellasega, you have had input from some of the best professionals in the country and they haven't been able to help your daughter. What makes you think we have answers?"

I remember his words when letters from people whose lives have been changed forever by eating disorders come across my desk. These communications arrive all too frequently because I am a parent who shared stories of mothers caring for struggling teens in my first book (*Surviving Ophelia: Mothers Share Their Wisdom of the Tumultuous Teenage Years*). Clearly, reading about the experiences of others provided support for family members all around the world who were confused and anxious about what was happening to their daughters. I discovered that sometimes, support is all that can be offered.

That's what this book is all about.

Over the course of the last four years I have talked with dozens of mothers and fathers who volunteered to share experiences of caring for a child with anorexia, bulimia, or compulsive overeating. Like me and my husband, these parents questioned why such a thing had happened, and what they might have done wrong in raising their children. More importantly, they wanted to know how they could support their daughters or sons physically and emotionally.

Late one night when I was too consumed with anxiety about my daughter to sleep, I remembered some of the comforting and practical things mothers and fathers had told me over the years. Although I was sitting alone in my living room at two in the morning, I felt an amazing sense of peace as I recalled their words of wisdom. That gift of support from families who had coped with eating disorders was one that helped me persist through many hard times, and provided the insights that prompted this book. I realized most guides available for parents were written by therapists or doctors and that the "voice" of moms and dads, so notably absent, seemed like a critical piece of the caregiving puzzle!

Committed to developing a resource for families three years ago, I began to gather material in a more systematic way. First, I developed a simple survey that forty caregiving parents from across the country volunteered to answer. Often, their responses were annotated with lengthy comments, and many had letters attached providing additional information. Clearly, parents had a lot more to say than I expected, and felt strongly about their caregiving experiences.

To learn more, I scheduled a series of lengthy interviews with 26 mothers and fathers, again from a wide geographic area. I deliberately sought out parents of sons with eating disorders, as I felt their experiences were important to include. Over the course of several months, I asked these volunteers to answer a set of standard questions, and then to provide any additional comments they thought were relevant. The results of those efforts are contained in the pages that follow. To the best of my knowledge, no other book describes the firsthand experiences of such a large group of mothers and fathers who are caregivers for both sons and daughters. Two husband-wife teams offered interesting insights on how perspectives may differ with gender.

The children these parents provided care for ranged in age from 12 to 44, and while anorexia was the most common presenting feature, bulimia had affected half at some point (many children with anorexia also had used bulimic behaviors). Some children had been in recovery for years, while others were still in the acute phase of their eating disorder.

As is true with any study, people who volunteer to participate may not be typical of the larger population. Mothers and fathers who were even more stressed than the ones I talked to probably didn't have the mental or physical energy to spend an hour or more completing a questionnaire or being interviewed by me. Those who were less stressed may have thought their input wasn't relevant. The parents who did consent to interviews may have done so because they had a particular complaint or issue they wanted to speak about. That's not my impression, though. The things they shared resonated with my experiences, and with those of the many caregiving parents I've met.

Everyone I communicated with described the consolation they found through connection with other parents who had lived with anorexia or bulimia. A mother expressed it well: "Once I started talking to other people I realized my daughter had the same behaviors as their child, and I didn't feel so all alone."

Unfortunately, locating others who can and will share their joys and sorrows with you is not always as easy as looking in the newspaper for a support group. Some people don't feel comfortable seeking out or sitting with strangers and discussing deeply personal experiences. Others have unique geographic or personal circumstances that make it difficult to meet or converse in person.

This book is designed to overcome those obstacles and to provide parents with an easily accessible guide that originates from moms and dads just like them. Although neither the contributors nor the children they care for are identified by name, I wish to acknowledge their role in creating this resource. Readers may never be able to tell them how much support their stories provided, but in their hearts they know how much their words are appreciated. At one point, they longed for the same thing.

"Thank you for talking to parents, and for recognizing that we aren't pathological monsters who created this problem," one mother told me.

"Anything I can do to help, I will," said a father.

To protect the privacy of participants and their children and to summarize the large volume of information collected, I have used the transcripts and narratives to create miniature case studies that summarize what I was told, and to introduce and illustrate the points in each chapter.

It's important to realize that the material in this book is based on the thoughts and opinions of parents. Their experiences and feelings may be more or less relevant for you, and in no way should their comments be construed as medical advice. Rather, use this book in the same way you might a real-time support group: to obtain help in your role as a caregiver (or supporter of a caregiver) for a child with anorexia or bulimia.

When your child has an eating disorder, the sense of powerlessness can be so overwhelming it renders you into a state of paralysis or panic. In reality, there are many ways in which you can be of help. You are the person who has the unique ability to provide the "big picture" of your child's status that otherwise wouldn't be available to clinicians. As a parent, you are the expert on your child's lifelong health and illness issues in a way a doctor, nurse, or therapist can never be. While none of the information in this book is meant to substitute for care prescribed by licensed professionals, it is meant to show you how other mothers and fathers coped in a circumstance similar to yours, and made meaningful contributions to their child's care.

I know. I've been there. Like every mom I spoke to, I've lived with grief and guilt, and I've measured my days not in hours but in efforts made to support my daughter. Although this book isn't about my family, much of the information I received from parents was similar to my own caregiving experiences.

In the end, the greatest gift we can give each other is our stories. They offer the recognition, caring, and sharing that is so essential for others struggling individually and as a group to battle anorexia, bulimia, and other eating disorders.

1
Any Child, Any Time, Anywhere

꙳

"MY DAUGHTER COULD NEVER GET
AN EATING DISORDER. SHE LOVES TO EAT!" ~ A MOM

Larry and Kate North met during their junior year of college: she was an elementary education major, and he was on his way to dental school. For a year they had fun dating, spending their weekends exploring the big city where their college was located or being part of activities on campus. During school breaks, they traveled to visit friends and family throughout the country, often camping out in Larry's pup tent to save money.

When their senior year began, both realized if the relationship was to continue they needed to plan ahead. That Christmas, Kate saw something in her stocking that was the size and shape of an engagement ring box. When she opened it, her family got to witness Larry proposing, and her formal acceptance.

Spring semester went by quickly, crammed full of studies, wedding plans, a job search for Kate, and preparing for dental school for Larry. They married in May shortly after graduation and honeymooned with a leisurely camping trip in the Rocky Mountains whose memories quickly receded as they plunged into their new lives.

Kate taught fifth grade in a public school as Larry made his way through dental training. Both of the Norths wanted to keep their educational loans to a minimum, so in addition to teaching, Kate waitressed on the weekends and in the summer, and Larry worked in the dental school library as often as he could. When Kate unexpectedly got pregnant during Larry's third year of graduate school, they were both delighted and worried. How would they afford a baby?

Their fears dissolved the instant they saw Alicia. Whatever it took to give her a good life, Kate and Larry were determined to do it. During Larry's last year of school, Kate worked two part time jobs, juggling schedules with her husband so Alicia wouldn't have to be in day care for more than a few hours. Each of them read dozens of parenting books and conferred with each other on every child rearing decision.

It was an exhausting but exhilarating time: Larry was working hard and had an offer to join a four person practice in town as soon as he finished school. Kate spent the most time with Alicia, squeezing in substitute teaching and tutoring whenever she could. Both of them knew their situation was tough, but temporary.

Each new accomplishment their baby daughter made gave Larry and Kate the energy to persevere. Although they had $50,000 to pay off in educational loans, when Larry finished dental school they eagerly anticipated the beginning of a new phase of life.

Their son Noel was born close to the sixth anniversary of Larry's marriage proposal, which prompted them to decide it was time to move out of their tiny apartment. Kate's parents intervened, insisting on giving the parents of their only grandchildren enough money for a down payment on a house.

Although Kate's teaching experience had left her intimidated by the thought of being surrounded by children all day, every day, she loved being a "stay at home" mom. Alicia and Noel were both outgoing children, each in a different way. Alicia was talkative and social: by kindergarten she already had a large circle of friends. Noel was physical and athletic, interacting with other boys through sports or action games.

The early parenting years for the Norths became predictable. Larry guarded his weekend time when he wasn't on call so the family could take camping trips; he had given up his beloved tent for a bigger model. Holidays were spent with family, and every summer the entire family went to the beach for a week. On Sundays, Kate took the children to the local Catholic church, and Larry made sure they visited synagogue with him on a regular basis.

Alicia and Noel got along as well as any other siblings the Norths knew of. For the most part, Larry and Kate remained as compatible as they had in their dating years, looking forward to pitching their tent and cooking outdoors whenever they could get away. Their only disagreements were about money (Larry was anxious to pay off the last of their loans and begin saving for the children's college while Kate preferred to fix up their new home) and occasionally, religion. They compromised on both accounts.

While Kate had thought she would go back to teaching once Alicia and Noel were in first grade, her life quickly filled up with volunteer activities: committees at school and church, working on the records at a small clinic for low income children where Larry provided free dental care twice a month, and ferrying the children to their many activities. She had several groups of women friends: one from her neighborhood to walk with every morning, one from the school that she worked on projects with, and another from church. She couldn't imagine how she would squeeze eight hours of work into her already busy day.

Larry was doing well at his practice, and was proud of his family. He saw Kate as a pillar of the community with her volunteer work, and loved being "an assistant to the assistant coach" of Noel's soccer team. When he read the newspaper after their evening meal, Alicia would often practice her piano in the family room, which made the time even more relaxing. He was sure she had enough talent to make a career of music if she chose to.

The middle school years weren't quite as smooth as the lower grades were for both Alicia and Noel. There were "girl problems" with Alicia's friends, and Noel was still immature physically, so he lagged behind the other boys in soccer. Kate made sure to be available almost every day after school as this was the time when her children often confided their upsets to her.

The summer after Alicia graduated from middle school both children were allowed to take a friend on their beach vacation for the first time. Walking on the boardwalk with Larry (who wore his "Soccer Dad" tee-shirt), Kate saw her children just ahead of them through different eyes. They were becoming more interested in spending time with friends, and no longer came to her with every problem.

"Things are changing," she said to Larry as they strolled, hand in hand, behind the four adolescents. He agreed with her, but was upbeat, as always.

"For the better, Katy, for the better."

ॐ

ALICIA AND NOEL were both good students, and had always competed fiercely to see who could bring home the best grades, an honor that switched back and forth from semester to semester. In all other ways, as they matured they continued to be so different no one would guess they were siblings.

One day as Kate cleaned the house she paused at her children's bedroom doors, struck by how much each room spoke for its owner. Alicia's CDs were stored alphabetically, and the books on her shelves were neatly arranged by size. In her closet, clothes were grouped in colors, and the stuffed animals on her bed always rested against a freshly fluffed pillow and smooth coverlet. In contrast, most of Noel's clothing was shoved under his bed, and his closet was crammed full of soccer balls, basketballs, shin guards, a bike helmet, and a skateboard.

The siblings were different in physical ways, too. Noel was a blue-eyed blond with a wiry build that usually stood him in good stead on the soccer field. Alicia's hair and eyes were dark, and while she'd always been average in height and weight, in middle school her body began to change. In comparison to her friends, who had already gotten their periods and filled out their bras, Alicia was pearshaped and flat-chested. Remembering how miserable she'd felt when her puberty lagged behind that of her peers, Kate tried to be reassuring and to focus her daughter on other accomplishments: her musical talent, her good grades, and the gang of girlfriends who were always ready to sleep over.

Freshman year in high school was rough for Alicia. She continued to compare her body to everyone else's with great dissatisfaction. When she insisted on buying a padded bra, Kate relented, but the first time Alicia wore it she came home in tears.

"The boys on the bus all made sneezing noises when I got on," she told her mother, explaining that this was a standard taunt for girls who were suspected of stuffing their bras with tissue.

Noel wasn't having an easy time in seventh grade, either. He didn't make the private league soccer team as he had hoped, which threw him into a slump for most of the fall. Despite his success at basketball later in the semester, he wanted to be with the soccer teammates he'd played with since grade school.

Larry spent time practicing lay-ups with Noel, and took Alicia out for "Father-Daughter" shopping trips where he would compliment whatever clothes she tried on. Kate checked in with her children daily, and called Dr. Grant, their pediatrician, to see if he had any advice about Alicia's slow development. He assured her Alicia would probably experience a sudden growth spurt which would resolve the problem.

By June, Kate was glad to see the school year end. There had been enough nagging problems to make her breathe a sigh of relief on the last day of exams. She and Larry planned to take Alicia and Noel to the beach for two weeks to reconnect and enjoy each other. Summer camps and other activities would hopefully help get them get back on track.

The summer did go well. Soccer camp improved Noel to the point of qualifying once more for the private team, and Alicia started her period and her breasts got noticeably bigger. Shopping for back to school clothes was fun that year because Alicia seemed to actually enjoy looking at her reflection in each new outfit.

In September, Alicia came home after a busy day in tenth grade and announced that her best friend Melanie had confessed that her older sister Carole, who was in college, had an eating disorder. After providing a vivid description of Carole's binging and purging behaviors, Melanie told Alicia that her sister had lost so much weight she looked like a different person. Kate knew Melanie and Carole's mother Rita, but hadn't heard her talk about any problems during their periodic get-togethers at the coffee shop. She made a mental note to ask about it discreetly the next time the two of them were alone. That conversation never occurred.

Toward the beginning of October, Larry asked if everything was okay with Alicia. Kate wondered why he was asking, since she hadn't noticed anything different than usual.

"When I went in her room to say goodnight, I leaned over to kiss her and my keys fell out of my shirt pocket, so I bent down to get them. Alicia grabbed for them, but not before I saw under her bed. There was all kinds of food there, Katy. Bags of potato chips, candy bars, I don't know where she got all that stuff, or why she would have it in her room." Larry was clearly concerned over what he'd seen.

"You're right, that is weird," Kate answered, thinking of Alicia's previous refusal to allow anyone to eat in her room because she didn't want crumbs on the floor. The next day when she asked Alicia about it, her daughter shrugged and said she wanted to make sure she had snacks available when she wanted them. Before her mother could respond, she hurried out the door to school.

Despite the hoard of snacks, Alicia's food intake seemed to be diminishing. Desserts were the first thing to go, even though she had always loved to help her mother bake cakes and cookies. Now, she watched her brother dunk homemade chocolate chip cookies in his milk with open disgust.

"Do you know how much fat you're stuffing in your body?" She would sneer. Noel would respond by opening his mouth to share a vision of partially chewed food with his sister.

On Friday nights the family traditionally ordered pizza, which was eaten in the family room while they all watched a series of sitcoms. Alicia usually had two or three hefty pieces, but now she limited herself to one, which she blotted carefully with a paper towel before eating.

"It's so greasy," she explained to her father.

Within a month of Larry discovering the stash of food, Kate was sure her daughter was losing weight. The pants that had fit snugly in September were looser, and the breasts Alicia had seemed so pleased with shrank under the baggy sweatshirts and sweaters she wore nearly every day.

"Are you losing weight?" she asked one day as they drove to piano lessons.

Alicia smiled. "Why? Do I look thinner?"

"Yes, you do," her mother answered slowly, not sure of how much to push the issue. "So have you?"

"Maybe a few pounds, but it's not like I didn't need to."

Alicia flounced off to her piano lesson and didn't say anything else about her appearance, but when Kate checked the next day, all the same snacks were under the bed, untouched. That Thanksgiving, Alicia proposed packing her own meal to take to her grandparents' house where they would be celebrating, which set off alarm bells in Kate's head. Alicia had always loved the traditional dishes her parents served.

She called Dr. Grant and scheduled an appointment for as soon as possible. When the day came for the visit, Alicia was disgruntled over missing school, but what bothered Kate was her consumption of two diet sodas in the car as they drove to the office. When the nurse who admitted them to the clinic asked Alicia to step on the scale, she was outright uncooperative.

"Just get on the scale," Kate urged. When her daughter finally relented, the number on the balance was fifteen pounds lower than it had been the summer before.

Dr. Grant asked to see Alicia alone, and then called Kate in. He said he wasn't concerned about Alicia just yet, as she was just slightly under the bottom weight for her age group and height.

"She's been dieting, but she's promised she'll eat more now, right Alicia?"

Alicia nodded, and Kate wondered if Dr. Grant had classified her as a neurotic mother, given her previous call. She didn't mention the strange supply of snacks.

When Larry heard what had happened at the doctor's office, he was satisfied. "She'll start eating," he assured Kate, and the next evening, he brought home a half gallon of chocolate marshmallow ice cream, Alicia's favorite.

"Here you go, kiddo," he said, delivering a bowlful to her after everyone had finished their meals. "And young man, one for you." He gave Noel an equally generous serving.

Noel lost no time in eating his ice cream, but Alicia stirred hers until it was almost completely melted, then claimed she was too full to eat it. The same sequence occurred the next night, and the night after that.

It was clear to Kate that something was going on with Alicia. She seemed to have stopped smiling completely, and the only thing that interested her was what would be served for dinner each night. She grew so tired of Alicia hovering by her, checking containers of food and generally getting in the way while she cooked that she tried turning the meal preparation over to her. Alicia served such tasteless low fat food that Larry and Noel refused to eat it.

There seemed to be no end to Alicia's obsession with food. The less she ate of it, the more fascinated she became with copying recipes, calculating fat grams, and searching for new combinations of low calorie food. Kate began to find other food stashes in her daughter's room: jumbo packs of sugarless gum hidden in her closet, dozens of empty containers of low calorie breath mints under her bed, and a shoebox full of artificial sweetener.

Frustrated, she called a national organization that offered information on eating disorders and was directed to a website with signs and symptoms of anorexia. Although Kate had seen these signs and symptoms before, she hadn't systematically compared them with Alicia's behavior. As she sat down in front of the computer to compare symptoms, Kate found each of the questions seemed to be about her daughter. When she tallied more "yes" responses than "no" she realized the problem she had been reluctant to face was real.

She called Dr. Grant's office again, and he returned her call later that day. He listened to the update on Alicia, then asked a few questions about her medical status. When Kate had nothing tangible like dizzy spells or heart irregularities to report, he suggested she contact a therapist and take her daughter there.

"Can you suggest someone?" she pressed, but Dr. Grant deferred, saying he really didn't know any specialists in the area, leaving Kate frustrated.

Determined to find help, Kate spent most of the next day on the phone. She called every therapist in the phone book who claimed to treat adolescents, but discovered many would not take a child with anorexia or bulimia. Each one referred her on to Tia Reeves, a psychologist who had her own practice. Luckily, Tia had an opening for the following week, so Kate booked it for Alicia, and then talked with Larry about how to break the news to their daughter.

Things didn't go well when the two of them spoke to their daughter that evening. Larry explained their concerns, and Kate told her about the appointment. Instantly, Alicia exploded, insisting there was nothing wrong with her and screaming at her parents for their lack of understanding.

In the days that followed, Larry and Kate tried bribery and coercion to get their daughter to agree to the appointment, but neither worked. There was no reward meaningful enough and no punishment so serious that she would give in.

Finally, it was Melanie who made the difference. Kate had noticed Alicia's girlfriends rarely called anymore, and on weekends her daughter was always at home, watching television or sleeping. When Melanie showed up at their house the Saturday before the appointment, Kate was thrilled.

"We haven't seen you in so long!" she said, sweeping Alicia's friend indoors.

"Mrs. North, some of Alicia's friends and I wanted to talk to you. We're really concerned about her." Melanie was somber as she told Kate about the many meals Alicia skipped at school, and how difficult it seemed to be for her to pay attention in class. Several other classmates wanted to come over that evening and speak to Alicia.

Gratefully, Kate agreed. Melanie went upstairs to Alicia's bedroom for a few minutes, then returned to tell Kate everything was set: she would be back that evening with a group of girls who had been closest to Alicia. Larry and Kate were also invited.

The meeting was more effective than all of the North's pleading and threatening. Within five minutes of being gently but emotionally confronted by her friends, Alicia broke down crying and admitted her "dieting" had gotten out of control. Several of her friends were also in tears by the time she finished.

Kate had high hopes for the meeting with Tia, which Alicia agreed to attend after the visit from her friends. When they arrived, the therapist informed Kate that the first meeting would be mostly assessment. Then she took Alicia back to begin the process, leaving Kate in a waiting area.

For an hour, Kate sat in the waiting room, wondering what was going on behind the therapist's closed door. Finally, she was summoned inside and motioned to a seat.

"Mrs. North, your daughter meets all the criteria for anorexia nervosa," Tia announced, holding a sheaf of papers. "From what I gather, this has been going on for several months."

Kate was flooded with both relief and pain. Now she and Larry knew for sure what Alicia's problem was, but it was shocking to hear the truth, to wonder why such a thing had happened, and to know what to do next. When she asked Tia what had caused the anorexia, she was told that would be explored in the next therapy session. Before she could ask further questions, she and Alicia were ushered out the door.

"There's a parent support group that meets here on Wednesday evenings," Tia told Kate in lieu of good bye. "You might find it helpful."

From that point on, Kate and Larry became different parents, and the entire North family found their lives radically transformed by Alicia's anorexia. Going to the support group or talking to any of her friends about the situation felt too overwhelming for Kate at that point, so she searched the Internet for alternatives. She found information on several sites, and connected with a few mothers who began to email her helpful tips: "Don't fight about food. You'll never win that battle," said one. Another suggested she schedule a private appointment with Tia to discuss Alicia's situation.

Alicia continued to lose weight, despite continued visits to Tia, who refused Kate's request for an individual meeting as she felt it would violate Alicia's trust in her. Kate no longer walked with her friends or socialized because she was too busy worrying about Alicia and trying to find a source of help. When the school nurse called to report that Alicia's teacher had sent her down to be checked after she slept through an entire class, it seemed time to return to Dr. Grant.

This time the doctor was alarmed. Alicia had lost ten more pounds since her initial visit, and her heart rate was slow. He asked one of his technicians to draw some blood work, and instructed Kate to buy fluids laced with electrolytes for her daughter.

"I want to see you back tomorrow, but go to the Emergency Room immediately if Alicia has any cardiac symptoms or dizziness," he instructed. Thankful for Larry's medical background, Kate drove Alicia home, helping her out of the car and carefully tucking her in bed.

When they returned the next day, Dr. Grant had the results of Alicia's lab work and insisted that she be admitted to the hospital's psychiatric unit for observation. Kate was stunned, and asked why her daughter would go to a psychiatric unit when her physical health was the problem.

"Anorexia is primarily a psychiatric diagnosis, Mrs. North. Alicia needs to eat, and to eat now. The unit can provide support for her, and hopefully she'll comply, but if not, they can put a tube into her stomach and feed her that way."

Although Dr. Grant meant to soothe Kate and Alicia's upset, it did the opposite. Both mother and daughter were sobbing by the time he left the exam room to call the hospital.

Over the next two years, Alicia would be hospitalized many times. During one stay she did require the tube Dr. Grant mentioned in order to treat the state of malnutrition her anorexia had created. Initially, Alicia continued to see Tia for therapy when she wasn't hospitalized, but soon she began to complain to Kate about Tia and the sessions.

"She keeps insisting that I'm not telling her the truth about my past, but I am. There's nothing you or dad or anyone else did to cause my anorexia, but she keeps suggesting that's very likely the problem." Alicia repeated the same complaint again and again.

Since Kate also felt Tia had blamed her for Alicia's anorexia, she was not surprised to hear this, but she and Larry insisted the therapy continue until one session when Tia finally invited them to participate. During that hour, she told the Norths that their daughter was intimidated by them and feared what would happen if she expressed her true feelings about her parents. Tia was convinced repressed anger at Kate and Larry's attempts to control Alicia's life was the underlying reason for her anorexia.

Larry asked Tia how she could come to such a conclusion when she had never even spoken to him or Kate at length. He challenged her assumption that Alicia was upset with them. The tone of the session instantly turned hostile, with Tia insisting her impressions were correct, and Kate and Larry astonished to be blamed for their daughter's illness. Alicia sat silently through the exchanges between her parents and therapist, but afterwards she showed a glimpse of her former dry sense of humor.

"I hate to say 'I told you so' but…" she drawled from the back seat as they drove home. Larry and Kate looked at her and saw the glimmer of a smile on their daughter's face for the first time in many months. They all began to laugh and the tension in the car dissolved.

Kate searched for a new therapist, but ran into the same obstacles she'd confronted before. In desperation, she thought perhaps they should stick it out with Tia, who had to be better than no therapist at all. She was mulling this over in the grocery store when she ran into Rita, Melanie's mother.

It had been a long time since Kate had met any of her women friends for coffee, and when she went to church it was only for the service and not for the hospitality hour afterward, as she used to do.

Seeing Rita, she realized what had been lost in her life without the regular contact of her women friends. But what would she talk to them about? The latest antidepressant Dr. Grant ordered for Alicia? The empty boxes of laxatives she found in Alicia's trash can which made her worry her daughter was now purging as well as restricting? The arguments she and Larry had begun to have over how their daughter should be treated? And if she did voice any of her concerns, how would the other mothers respond to her?

As they chatted, Kate cautiously mentioned what she had heard about Carole, Rita's older daughter. Bluntly, Rita admitted that she'd "been through hell" when her daughter had been bulimic during her first year of college. Amazed, Kate asked many questions about how Rita had coped, and who had helped her. Rita suggested Kate come to her house for a few minutes after the grocery store, as she had some books and telephone numbers she would share.

That moment was another turning point for Kate. Rita's advice led her to a new therapist named Margie, a social worker who had facilitated the parent support group Rita attended. Margie was the opposite of Tia, including Kate and Larry from the start, and informing Alicia that the four of them were a team, and the purpose of the team was to defeat the anorexia.

Margie's therapy focused on separating Alicia from the anorexia, and stressing that neither medication nor counseling would work until a healthy nutritional state was achieved. She suggested weekly visits to a nutritionist that she knew well, and insisted that Kate and Larry attend at least one of the support group meetings.

Although Alicia ended up being treated as an inpatient one more time after that, Kate and Larry believe her recovery began when she connected with her new therapist. They also credit the eating disorder center where Alicia was referred for her final inpatient stay with sparking her motivation.

"What a difference," Kate said to Larry soon after they visited Alicia at the center. "Just think of what might have happened if someone had referred us there in the beginning."

She was referring to the range of specialized services their daughter received: a psychiatrist who worked only with eating disorders saw Alicia every other day, a nurse practitioner whose practice consisted solely of girls with anorexia or bulimia led a daily group and did individual therapy, and a nutritionist and art therapist were fulltime employees at the center. Best of all, families were included in an intensive psychoeducational program that recognized how stressful eating disorders were for everyone involved. Although the program was expensive and the Norths had to take out a loan to pay for it because it wasn't a service their insurance plan covered, they felt it was a place where Alicia would get the right treatment.

During the center's family program Kate and Larry also learned of Noel's true feelings. For the years of Alicia's illness he had been put "on the backburner" again and again. He told his parents in a special therapy session that their only focus was Alicia, and that he was tired of having neighbors drive him to and from soccer practice and games.

Hearing his son's words brought tears to Larry's eyes. Kate tried to hug Noel and apologize for what seemed like neglect, but he pushed her away. It was Alicia who finally got through to him, hanging her head and saying her brother was right. She had been the focus, and she recognized how selfish her behavior had been.

The center's therapist jumped in at that point to stress that the session wasn't about blame, but to look at ways in which the family could function better. Together, they created a plan that would keep Alicia safe and give Noel more attention.

During the family program, Kate finally received an answer to a question that had plagued her since the onset of Alicia's eating problems: "Why did you gather up all that snack food and hide it under your bed?"

Alicia looked sheepish. "I wanted to have it there in case I did decide to eat it, but not eating it when it was right there made me feel strong, like I was in control of my willpower."

After being discharged from the center and returning to therapy with Margie, the Norths noticed that Alicia began to surrender her eating disorder behaviors bit by bit. Sometimes, she would have trouble for a day or two and they would think she was slipping back to acute anorexia, but slowly, she progressed toward recovery.

By the time Alicia was a senior in high school, the Norths had gone on their first family vacation in two years, and were regularly attending Noel's soccer matches. Alicia was spending time with her friends on the weekends, and had started mending her relationship with her brother. Larry was back as a helper coach, and Kate had begun to meet Rita and other friends for coffee on a regular basis. She was even thinking of returning to a teaching job once Noel finished high school.

The Norths were worried about what would happen when Alicia began college, but Margie encouraged them all to work day to day on recovering before any long term decisions were made. She pointed out that Alicia was a bright girl who could go to college at any time but that the immediate priority was maintaining her health.

Hearing Margie's feedback, Kate nodded in agreement, thankful that they had found someone who had tried to be helpful not only to Alicia but the entire family. Kate realized that little by little, she, Larry, and Noel were on a journey too, traveling alongside Alicia and trying to stay on the sometimes twisting path that would eventually lead to recovery.

Section One

❧❧

Say It Isn't So:
The Eating Disorder Bomb

2
The Job You Never Wanted

శ్రీఆశ

"IT'S LIKE HAVING A TODDLER,
EXCEPT SHE'S EIGHTEEN."
DAD OF A GIRL WITH ACUTE ANOREXIA

Nan, a single mom, didn't know where to go when her
family doctor suggested that her only daughter Denise
had developed anorexia at age thirteen. The two of them lived
in a small town in California where the nearest source of
specialized help was hours away. Although she was a registered
nurse, all the preparation and guidance Nan had received from
books and classes were of little help.

Instead, Nan learned what she really needed to know to
help Denise from Linda, a woman in her community she had
worked with on a school fundraiser many years before. When
her head nurse noticed that Nan seemed preoccupied and
worried at work and learned the reason why, she mentioned
Linda, her neighbor, the mother of a girl who had overcome
anorexia after years of struggle.

"I'm sure she wouldn't mind if you called," Nan's boss
said.

That night, Nan looked up Linda's phone number, and
dialed it with shaking fingers.

"You probably don't remember me, but would you be willing to answer a few questions?" she asked when Linda answered.

As soon as she learned why Nan was calling, Linda suggested they go for a quick cup of coffee the next day after work. The two women talked for an hour that afternoon, exchanging phone numbers and email addresses and arranging to meet again.

"She understood instantly what I needed most," Nan says now. "Not so much the name of a particular doctor or therapist, but a 'next step' to help Denise. She told me how things had gone for her and her daughter early on, and what she would have done differently, and it was a tremendous help. It turned out there was a therapist in town who had experience working with girls like Denise."

In the months that followed, Nan's "mentor" gave her the kind of advice she never found in books:

"Tell everyone around Denise not to focus on food. Give them suggestions of other 'safe' topics to distract her whenever she brings up the subject."

"Try and get the school to work with you to develop a plan for the day time. The guidance counselor helped me put a number of things in place like periodic updates from the teachers and school nurse, and meal support when my daughter would accept it."

"Be prepared for your kitchen to turn into a battleground."

Linda described the tensions that occurred in her home as her ill daughter's siblings attempted out of desperation and panic to try to get their sister to eat. Although Nan didn't have other children, she nonetheless recognized some of the same dynamics in her parents and sisters as they took on similar roles with Denise.

Often, Linda called Nan to see how she was doing, and more than once, her insights and experience gave Nan a head start in finding specific treatments. She was the person Nan turned to when Denise's weight dropped dangerously low, leading to a hospital admission. She was the one who listened for hours on the telephone as Nan questioned why this had happened and how she would ever be able to cope with it.

"You just have to persevere, and know that whether Denise tells you or not, the things you do matter. If it weren't for you, Denise wouldn't be able to come home from the hospital so quickly," Linda told Nan.

Linda went on to describe how she felt pressured to leave her job when her daughter had developed anorexia in eighth grade: "Every week there were four visits: the doctor, the nutritionist, the therapist, and the psychiatrist. How could I have run her to all those appointments and held down a fulltime job?"

Linda recognized that she was lucky to have a husband whose fulltime income and insurance benefits permitted her to stop work because of her daughter's needs. It was hard to imagine the struggle Nan faced as a single parent. Still, she could help Nan locate resources and save her dozens of phone calls in the search for help. With that and the assistance of her elderly parents and a set of sisters who didn't really understand why Denise was refusing to eat, Nan got by.

"I simply would not have survived without Linda," Nan says now. "She gave me the support and understanding even my family couldn't offer, and since her daughter had recovered, she always held out that precious ray of hope. Denise and I are both indebted to her."

It's a Family Affair

Eating disorders harm both patients and parents. Perhaps it's because at the moment of a child's birth most parents instantly feel an unspoken and overpowering commitment to nourish and support their sons or daughters for the rest of their lives. From that point on, the provision of emotional and physical "food" continues to be one of the strongest ties connecting mothers and fathers to their children.

Food is significant beyond the context of the immediate family, too. Our culture is one that emphasizes the sharing of traditional dishes on occasions happy and somber: birthdays, holidays, funerals, and other religious ceremonies involve food as well as family. Both the calories we consume and the feelings we experience while doing so can provide a connection between unrelated individuals in cafeterias, restaurants, street corners, and grocery stores.

The power of food and its place in the function of every family becomes painfully apparent when a daughter or a son develops an eating disorder. While an excess or deficit of calories may seem to be the most apparent issue, what is deeper, more significant, and perhaps most stressful is the blow that is dealt to the parent-child relationship.

When someone you love eats too little or too much, his or her rejection of both physical and emotional nurturing strikes at the heart of what parenting is all about. You may even question your ability to perform the most basic role of "providing for" your child.

But families are critical. No medication, counselor, nurse, or physician can replace living arrangements that enable a child to hang on and keep battling illness during the 23 hours of the day when he or she is not in therapy. Long after the clinics have closed and the physicians have gone home, moms and dads are at home with their ill sons or daughters, unsure of what to do next.

How can you cope with the uncertainty of eating disorders? Is there ever a way to overcome the fear that your child will die, or live with permanent damage? As with so many other health conditions, the help offered by professionals or books often doesn't answer those daunting questions. It's the caregiving experts — people who have lived with the disease day in and day out — who can offer practical sensibilities that will help you function long after the doctor's office is closed and the therapy sessions have ended.

In reality, eating disorder care, like every other chronic illness, is family care. Without the day-to-day support of mothers and fathers, the recovery rates are likely to be much lower.

The True Challenge
The struggle for caregivers like Nan is not to get a certain number of calories in the child every day, but to create and maintain an emotional environment where an ill son or daughter is safe and willing to take in sustenance. It's one of the most demanding jobs a parent can ever face, and the burden of providing this kind of care is significant.

Although Nan had only Denise at home to consider, for other families with two parents and multiple siblings, the impact can be even more profound. As Linda pointed out, every meal can be a struggle, and dinner time, a routine that traditionally symbolizes family togetherness, can turn the dining room table into a war zone.

Insidiously, a son or daughter's distorted relationship with food can start a chain reaction that challenges the function of every member of the family. Mothers and fathers stop talking about their child's regular activities such as school and sports, and begin focusing on how many calories are or are not consumed. Siblings grow to resent the time and energy their parents have to divert away from them and toward the sick individual. The focus on food can be painful for everyone.

Wearing Out

Mothers and fathers feel physically and mentally exhausted by the ongoing demands involved in monitoring and caring for their ill child. They can have trouble sleeping due to anxiety, and their job performance is often hampered by distraction. Perhaps the most difficult thing to accept is the hopelessness and lack of control that accompanies this kind of caregiving.

At the same time, a team of health care providers — previously strangers — becomes intimately involved with the family, sometimes seeming to supplant parents as the primary support system for a struggling child. Often, these experts scrutinize minutiae of family life that would have, in other circumstances, seemed unremarkable.

In Nan's case, her five year old divorce from Denise's father, who was an absentee parent, took on new significance as a therapist delved into the past. Her failure to remarry and the singular nature of her relationship with Denise was also commented on in family therapy.

Nan felt these remarks like physical blows, since single parenting had left her isolated and afraid, despite Linda's support. Why hadn't anyone noticed that Denise's father had dropped out of her life at age eight and never returned? Why weren't negative statements balanced with a recognition that she was devoting every free minute she had to helping her daughter?

Desperate to Help

Nan, like Linda and so many others, was committed to doing anything and everything in her power to help her child. "I feel I've lost her," "She's gone away," and "The child I once knew is like a stranger," are all statements from parents who have a child suffering from an eating disorder. The sense of loss that occurs when anorexia or bulimia consumes the life of someone you love deeply can be truly overwhelming, and the desire to help is so strong parents literally put their lives on hold. Guilt and grief become the fuel that enables parents to persist in almost superhuman efforts to help their child.

"For a long time I felt sick to my stomach and then I began to get mad. I kept trying to talk to my son in a caring manner. It was very hard not to blame myself for this," the mom of a son with bulimia said.

Given the reluctance of health insurance companies to reimburse for services unless a child is close to death (a huge stressor), the reality of care for sons and daughters with eating disorders is that mothers and fathers are at the forefront of offering support, 24/7. The everyday tasks of caretaking can become almost too much to handle: providing emotional support, comfort, and a secure environment along with tending to more concrete tasks like meal preparation and clinic appointments. Nonetheless, parents are eager to do whatever it takes to help their children.

The Parenting Price Tag

Again and again, parents told me that caring for a child with an eating disorder was the most stressful situation they had ever confronted. Difficulties in finding care, interactions with the treatment team, dealing with the child's denial and food-related behaviors, and providing emotional, physical, and financial support on a day-to-day basis top the list of challenges. Although mothers and fathers are relieved to have ways to help their ill children, the "cost" of caregiving is tremendous: my previous research showed that a statistically significant decline occurred in the mental and physical health of *mothers* over the course of their children's eating disorders.

The financial impact can also be profound: one family spent over a thousand dollars a month on costs not covered by insurance. These "out of pocket" expenses accumulate as parents purchase special foods, pay deductibles for therapy and medicine, and take time off work to drive their children to appointments.

Acknowledging the stress of caregiving and finding ways to help families help their sons and daughters with anorexia or bulimia is no trivial endeavor. It's no longer unusual to see girls in outpatient treatment with feeding tubes because they aren't "ill" enough to be hospitalized. Who purchases the expensive feedings required for use with a tube, and who provides the back up care should anything go wrong? The family. Who buys the prescribed medicines, and who makes sure they are taken? Again, families do. All the therapeutic meal plans developed by the best nutritionists in the world are useless if there isn't someone to obtain and help prepare the food for a child too sick to do it alone.

As of 2004, the incidence of eating disorders continues to climb as does the number of books on treatment written by both patients and professionals. Many experts offer checklists and step-by-step strategies for helping, along with facts and opinions. None contain the collective wisdom of parents who have provided around the clock support for children with eating disorders for months and even years — the missing information that can help families.

The psychiatrist who told me there are few answers is right, but there are things that can be done to encourage and sustain families who have a member in the throes of anorexia, bulimia, or another eating problem. Knowing that you are not alone, gaining information on what might come, clarifying your role, and receiving guidance from those who have lived day-to-day with a child who suffers can't make life easy, but can make it *easier.*

Down and Then Back Up

Although many parents thought eating disorders could simply be cured once they were diagnosed, in reality the route to recovery is almost always long and arduous. In fact, the entire course of anorexia or bulimia is much more of a process than a single point in time when a diagnosis is made. Usually, an initial concern escalates as the child's status declines. Eventually, the discovery process leads to an "official" diagnosis and, hopefully, active treatment. From there, improvement occurs gradually and often in tandem with setbacks.

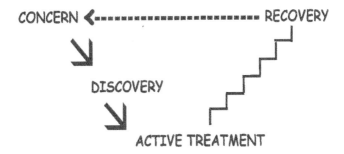

On learning of their children's illnesses, mothers responded much as Nan did, feeling they had failed their children, and blaming themselves for the eating disorder. One told me she came to this conclusion after a family therapy session. "Their message was, you've screwed up this child hopelessly," she shared.

Others described feeling sad and guilty because of their own perceptions of parenting.

"Mothers take care of you. They make you better. I haven't done that for her," explained an interviewee, who reflected what several women expressed.

Unfortunately, as treatment begins, both mothers and fathers often find themselves in a double bind situation, negatively labeled by health care professionals and a source of anger and resentment from a child who irrationally views them as the enemy. Even families who may have contributed to the eating problem don't benefit from being judged or blamed because parenting does not stop when a child develops an eating disorder. If anything, it intensifies.

"It seemed like the struggles would never end," one parent told me, and another said there was no "light at the end of the tunnel" during the acute phase of the eating disorder. For some families this phase was as short as a few months; for others it took years.

However, the good news is that some form of recovery occurred for most children. When a complete turnaround took place, it was often a dramatic event that could not be explained, and happened suddenly. More common was a slow but steady progress toward health: improved awareness, better eating habits, and an interest in education, job, or relationships that did not involve food. There were setbacks and plateaus, and relapses often started the cycle over, but recovery was like an uphill climb out of a dark and scary hole that sometimes seemed bottomless.

Help Wanted

Caregiving for an ill child is a career, a significant life experience you never asked for, and would prefer to do without. Can you imagine what a job description for this kind of work would look like?

> WANTED: MOTHER OR FATHER WILLING TO BE AVAILABLE AROUND-THE-CLOCK FOR ACUTELY ILL CHILD. WEEKENDS AND HOLIDAYS ARE A MUST. DUTIES VARY FROM DAY-TO-DAY SO FLEXIBILITY IS ESSENTIAL. RESPONSIBILITIES MAY INCLUDE BUT ARE NOT LIMITED TO: MONITORING, TRANSPORTING, COUNSELING, SUPERVISING, AND COORDINATING CARE FOR A SERIOUSLY ILL SON OR DAUGHTER. NOTE: THIS IS AN UNPAID (VOLUNTEER) POSITION.

Although it seems like a grueling and thankless endeavor, the picture is not completely bleak. Like so many of the difficult experiences that challenge us and pull forth strengths we may never realize we have, caregiving refines and reinforces our ability to persist in adverse circumstances, our creativity to marshal resources, and, most of all, our love for our children.

RESOURCES

Visit www.starvingfamily.com to join in an online message board discussion with other family members caring for someone with an eating disorder.

3
Discovery:
I Really Didn't Know

᪥᪥

"SHE'S BECOME VERY SECRETIVE LATELY, AND WE CAN'T SEEM TO HAVE A CIVIL CONVERSATION ABOUT ANYTHING. HER WEIGHT IS DROPPING TOO, ALTHOUGH SHE SNAPS AT ME WHEN I EVEN HINT THERE MIGHT BE SOMETHING WRONG WITH HER EATING." *E-MAIL FROM THE PARENT OF A THIRTEEN YEAR OLD GIRL*

"I WAS A BASKET CASE. SHE WAS DISAPPEARING RIGHT BEFORE MY EYES." *MOTHER OF TEENAGED GIRL WITH ANOREXIA*

Stacy Goode was an outgoing fourteen year old who lived with both her parents and her older sister Megan in a pleasant neighborhood she'd grown up in. As a freshman in high school, she developed an interest in running at Megan's prompting. Both girls planned to join the track team in the spring: Megan as the returning superstar and Stacy as a rising newcomer.

As the snow melted and the weather warmed, both girls went on practice runs every weekend and worked with weights in their basement exercise room. Megan, a state championship sprinter, shared her training strategies with Stacy, and gave her younger sister plenty of praise for quick learning. It was a bittersweet experience for both of them because in the summer, Megan, who was a senior, would graduate and leave for an early start in the college where she had been offered a cross country scholarship.

"My little sister is going to carry on the Goode tradition," she informed the track coach on the first day of practice. One of the senior boys jokingly told Stacy those would be "big shoes to fill" since Megan wore a size eleven sneaker.

As the season began and practice intensified, Stacy worked harder and harder to accomplish the same things her older sister had during freshman year: a starting position and expertise in the hurdles. Unfortunately, Stacy was short and muscular, like their father while Megan was tall and slender like their mother, with long legs that made her a natural runner.

Believing her performance would improve if she lost weight, Stacy began to change her food intake. Initially, her mother Gloria was not alarmed because she felt Stacy tended to eat too many snack foods. Seeing her push away desserts in favor of an apple was a positive change, and when the first few pounds dropped from her younger daughter's frame, Gloria complimented her.

"You are really getting in shape," she remarked, going on to praise Stacy's dedication to track. Mark, Stacy's father, also voiced his approval of her new interest in sports.

Then, without warning, Stacy's body broke down a month after track season had started, and she began to suffer from severe shin splints, ending up in tears every time she ran. Her place on the team slipped from among the fastest to one of the slowest, but her determination to lose weight continued because she believed being "fat" was the reason for her decline.

Now when Gloria looked at Stacy she saw a thin girl who came home from school and went directly to the living room where she turned the television on to a cooking show. For most of the evening, she stayed on the sofa, occasionally rising to fetch a glass of ice chips to chew.

"I think you've lost enough weight, Stacy," Gloria told her one night as she gave her a hug at bedtime. "In fact, I'm worried about you. Are you eating enough?"

Stacy adamantly denied that she was restricting her intake, but in the week that followed, she refused to eat dinner with her family, saying she'd had a large lunch at school, or wasn't hungry. When Mark insisted that she join them at the table, she sat down and rearranged the food on her plate while the others ate. At Gloria's insistence, she took a few bites.

The phone had stopped ringing for Stacy, too, and she rarely talked about her friends. Instead of going out shopping or to movies with girls from the neighborhood on weekends, she stayed at home, reading cookbooks in front of the food channel.

Gloria became consumed with worry. Nightly, she spoke to Mark about her latest observations, and even asked Megan to "spy" on her sister's behavior during school. At first, Mark and Megan exchanged knowing glances, rolling their eyes whenever Gloria verbalized her concerns, but soon, they too were on the alert, recognizing that both Stacy's weight and her behavior had undergone a dramatic change.

"Mom, you'd better do something," Megan urged one day after school. "During lunch today I saw Stacy dressed in her running clothes, going out to the track. I watched her start running, and went out to ask when she was going to eat lunch.

She told me she had a big breakfast at school and was skipping lunch, but I drove her to school, and I knew she was lying. We were late, and she went right to class."

In the Beginning

Almost every self help book on eating disorders I've seen begins with a chapter titled something like "Diagnosis" where all the signs and symptoms of an eating disorder are spelled out, along with statistics on anorexia and bulimia.

In real life, the point of "diagnosis" is much more of a process which begins with the first suspicions, and ends with a problem being identified. I call this process "Discovery."

Discovery is rarely as straightforward as a doctor's appointment where key criteria are identified and tallied. Instead, the path from perceiving that a problem might exist to the point of having it identified and treated by professionals is most often long, complicated by developmental stage of the child, and undermined by a societal sanction of thinness.

The Stage is Set

In the cases studied, many moms recalled an athletic event that created a context ripe for anorexia or bulimia. In one scenario, a child (like Stacy) would begin participating in a sport. When girls began to lose weight and develop muscle, others freely commented on how good they looked, which reinforced the many stereotyped messages young women were already getting about their bodies. Spurred on by a desire to excel, they would continue losing weight until their restricting of intake spiraled so out of control they no longer felt hungry.

For others who had to stop participating in a sport due to injury, fear of weight gain seemed to provide the same kind of trigger. In both situations, a girl's body image or her perception of it changed, and a trajectory of disordered eating began that took on a life of its own.

These responses suggest that some of these girls shared Stacy's perception that athletic performance improved with weight loss or a decrease in body fat. That one erroneous belief was all it took to trigger a weight loss cycle that evolved into a blatant eating disorder. For others, being complimented for losing weight rather than for athletic achievement seeded the eating disorder.

Boys seemed to arrive at bulimia and anorexia in a different way, although my sample of sons was much smaller. Teasing from peers and childhood weight problems that persisted in the high school years was the catalyst identified by several parents. Said one dad: "I mean here you are in a culture of jocks, guys with six pack abs and athletics the premier activity for boys. If you're chunky, even a little overweight, you are suddenly on the outside. Although my son wouldn't admit that it bothered him, I heard what his friends said to him when he was at his heaviest point, and it was all about his 'blubber.'"

There's Nothing Wrong!

No parent recalled their child readily admitting there was something wrong during the Discovery phase. All too often, the combination of a child's vehement denial and every parent's wish for their child to be happy and healthy made the "pre-diagnosis" period an especially rocky one.

Like Gloria, mothers frequently were the first to notice that something about their child was changing. Intuitively, some sensed a subtle shift in mood. Others saw food behaviors that concerned them. When these observations were voiced, they often met with fierce and even angry rebuttals from the child. Sometimes, other family members supported the child in negating a parent's concern. A father who chastised his wife for believing their youngest child was purging says: "I told her I didn't see any problem, and when our daughter insisted she wasn't throwing up, I believed her. Now I feel really bad about believing her lies over my wife's suspicions. Maybe if I had supported my wife, things would have gone differently."

In a separate interview, this man's wife described her feelings of frustration when her escalating worries were dismissed by both her husband and her daughter; months later she still feels traumatized by being placed in the role of "bad guy." She admits, though, that their responses to her were, on some level, a relief: "I didn't accept them, of course — but they delayed having to think there was a serious problem. After all, who goes out looking for things that are wrong with your child?"

Too Much, Not Enough

Eating was the behavior that most often attracted a parent's attention. Usually, there were only slight shifts in the beginning of the eating disorder: meals would be skipped, the child would claim not to be hungry, or food intake would change.

"She would avoid eating," was how one mother described it. "At first it was just that she had a big lunch, or she had already eaten. Then it progressed to pretending not to feel well and going to her room. Eventually she said she just wasn't hungry, and wouldn't take a bite."

"She used to calculate the calorie and fat content of every bite she ate," another mother recalled noticing early on.

"After every meal, she dashed to the bathroom," describes the dad of a girl with bulimia.

As eating became more impaired, a parent's concern escalated too. Again, any attempt to discuss the situation usually met with resistance from the child. Sometimes, these attempts prompted not only denial but anger:

"I confronted her about her weight loss, gently at first, asking her if she was feeling okay. Then, as the pounds kept dropping off, I got more direct and said she was getting too thin. She told me I was jealous, and denied any problem at all."

When a child was bulimic, weight loss may not have occurred or binging or purging may not have been obvious, but mothers still had a sense of something not right. They said:

"She went to the bathroom a lot. After awhile, I started to stand outside and listen, but she always ran water so I couldn't hear," or:

"He had special foods he always ate, and I noticed this. Later I realized it was food he could throw up easily."

Another mom who labeled her child an "exercise bulimic" recalled the "point of no return" for her: she found her daughter doing hundreds of sit-ups and jumping jacks every day, even though her energy was waning. She said: "It was something she was driven to do, almost as if she didn't really want to. There was this resigned look on her face when she went upstairs every night."

Other obvious changes during the Discovery phase related to appearance. At first, there may have been a weight loss that seemed within a healthy range, but as too many pounds were lost, the child began to look ill. Skin, hair, teeth, and eyes showed outward manifestations of malnutrition. Parents said:

"Her hair lost its shine, and got really thin."

"There was this funny layer of hair all over her body, kind of like babies have." [This is in fact the same lanugo babies are born with, and is a soft downy covering of hair that helps provide warmth. See http://encyclopedia.thefree dictionary.com/anorexia%20Onervosa.]

"She wore baggy clothes all the time."

Despite the obsessive drive to attain thinness, many children hid their bodies, either wearing loose shirts and pants or layering on extra clothing. The latter served to both hide their weight loss and keep them warm, since loss of body fat can cause a child to feel cold, even on the hottest summer day.

Ironically, as the weight loss continued, the child would still receive external praise at the same time mothers were sounding the alarm bells. Even when children looked obviously unhealthy, people would make comments such as:

"You look so thin! How do you do it?"

"You're really getting down there," or

"Wow, you've really lost weight. I wish I could!"

A child's denial could persist for a long time, and ranged in intensity from early assertions that he or she was just pursuing a "healthy diet" to later insistence (sometimes violent) that nothing was wrong. This became a major obstacle to obtaining care, especially when a child was older. It also eroded family trust, and the secrecy around the eating disorder became a powerful reinforcer for the child.

One mother said: "I began to question my sanity. My daughter was telling me there was nothing wrong, her father said he didn't see any problem, and when I got her to the doctor's for her yearly exam, he told me her body was adjusting to a growth spurt."

Later, when this daughter's anorexia became more apparent but the diagnosis still hadn't been officially established, the same mother recalls: "I told her we were going back to the doctor, and we were going to get to the bottom of this. She threw a bowl of salad against the wall and ran out of the house in anger. It was as if she was somehow 'protecting' her eating disorder, and sensed that we would soon have grounds to force her to get help."

Red Alert

To compensate for the concern that their child might be struggling with eating issues, mothers monitored both nutritional intake and emotional health more closely. Special foods were prepared, verbal encouragement to eat was given, and there were frequent check-ins on the child's overall well-being. In many ways, these activities created more anxiety, because they failed to make the child "better" and led to a further conviction that something was seriously wrong. "Be aware that you might not get quick answers about what's going on," was a frequent comment. "But don't give up on finding out. If you think something is wrong, something is wrong."

When their weight loss wasn't extreme and laboratory tests showed no chemical imbalance, physicians might opt for a "wait and see" approach, continuing to monitor the child's progress over a period of weeks or even months. This could be agonizing: a mother recalls watching her daughter lose forty pounds during the three months before her diagnosis and thinking: "We're going to lose her."

When this same mom took her daughter to the doctor, he didn't appreciate the level of her concern: "He [the pediatrician] was more like 'Oh, she'll be fine, she's just thin and has high metabolism' but I knew something was wrong big time."

Parents had some tips regarding actions a panicked mom or dad could take to help resolve ambiguity during the Discovery phase.

"Keep a diary," suggested one mother. "A factual record of your observations is going to mean more to a doctor than any emotional outpouring, although that's what you feel like doing." (The Starving Family Companion Workbook contains many forms designed for the purpose of assessment, record keeping, etc.) Most physicians and nurses welcome the opportunity to have this kind of information summarized and readily available to them during the brief time allotted to an office visit.

Another strategy suggested by parents is to begin informing yourself early in the process. "Learn all you can, both so you can help your child if needed, and so you can educate health care providers later," said one parent.

Although specialists, the Internet, and books were recognized as helpful sources, other parents were cited by far as the most credible way of obtaining information. Nearly everyone confirmed that individuals need to be very knowledgeable in order to deal effectively with health care providers.

Keeping Tabs

During the period when Gloria was waiting to see what the doctor would decide was wrong with Stacy, she and Mark responded to their daughter in ways I heard about again and again. They tried to encourage her to eat, monitored her intake, and tried to discuss whatever problems might be driving her to continue losing weight. Even Megan tried to help by "coaching" Stacy to eat, and trying to distract her from her focus on calories. Nonetheless, the efforts of the Goodes, like almost every other family, weren't successful and Stacy continued to decline, her weight dropping down, down, and down.

The challenge of discretely monitoring your child's behavior begins at a point long before professionals are involved and will be an activity that persists throughout the eating disorder. It can consume most of your waking time, whether you want it to or not: a parent's instinct to make sure his or her child is safe and thriving can blossom into an obsession during the Discovery phase.

As eating disorders persist, there is a delicate balance between being concerned and watchful versus hovering and overwhelming your child. Parents asked themselves questions in the Discovery stage that were repeated over and over again in later stages:

• How do I stay involved enough to show support and be of help to him or her without antagonizing or appearing over concerned?

- Am I reinforcing the problem by paying attention to it?
- At what point do I trust my intuition over input from others?

Bringing in the Back Ups

Sometimes, when parental influence wasn't enough, an intervention was needed to encourage the child to agree to be evaluated. "Her friends really helped, because they were saying the same things to her as I was," one mother recalled. Enlisting the support of others such as peers or relatives can be of benefit when confronting an older child, she suggested. (See the Intervention sidebar on the following page for more information.)

The Relief of Knowing

Getting to a diagnosis can be tricky when a child continues to deny that there's a problem, but it is vital to do so. Insurance reimbursement for health care and referrals to therapists can hinge on the diagnostic coding, so parents were even willing to go out of their prescribed reimbursement network to establish the presence of anorexia, bulimia, or ED-NOS ("eating disorder not otherwise specified").

"I paid five hundred dollars of my own to take her to a clinic where they diagnosed anorexia. We had reached a point where I was tired of her family doctor telling me there wasn't a problem, and since I didn't have a referral, the insurance company wouldn't pay for the visit," was an experience described by one mother.

The diagnostic process can be further complicated by unnecessary delays. Several parents shared their experiences of seeking help from doctors or therapists who lacked expertise

WHAT IS AN "INTERVENTION"?

An intervention is a caring way to bring an eating disorder (or other problem) out into the open. It can help the child recognize a need for change, and can marshal resources to accomplish this.

How do you know if your child needs an intervention?

Behavior
- Have there been recent changes in his or her behavior?
- Has school or job performance changed?
- Is there an unusual focus on food?
- Are relationships with friends still intact?

Conversation
- Is most of his/her conversation about food?
- Does the child talk about his/her appearance in a negative way?
- Are other comments made that suggest low self esteem?

Appearance
- Has there been a recent weight loss?
- Are there other physical changes in appearance?
- Does he or she wear baggy clothes or extra layers of clothes?

General mood
- Are there signs of depression (change in sleep, appetite, energy level)?
- Is he or she irritable?
- Has his or her mood changed suddenly?

If you find that you have seen many of these signs in your child and he or she won't admit to a problem, an Intervention might be the best "next step."

PREPARING FOR AN INTERVENTION

To prepare for an Intervention, gather together everyone who is important in the child's life. Have each person prepare to speak truthfully but lovingly to the child about his or her observations and concerns. As an option, you can include a coach, therapist, religious leader, or other adult who has a meaningful and caring connection to the child.

• Set a date and time for the intervention.
• Arrange for the child to arrive after everyone else has gathered.
• Hold the intervention in an environment that is emotionally "safe" for your child. Your home is probably best.
• Avoid any behavior that is threatening or demeaning to the child.
• "Rehearse" who will say what before the child arrives. As soon as the child arrives, reassure him or her of how important he or she is to each of you.
• Each person should stick to the facts in describing concerns, and speak calmly, even if the child gets emotional.
• Avoid "should's" or "ought's"
• Check in with how the child feels about what has been said, and what a "next step" might be.
• Stay with him or her after the intervention is over.

and failed to recognize an obvious problem. Others described a child's persistent refusal to seek help even when the illness could no longer be denied. When these things happened, the diagnosis didn't get made until the child was seriously ill and a crisis occurred.

In Stacy's case, Gloria set up an appointment early on with the pediatrician who had provided care to both of her daughters since childhood. He suggested biweekly visits to monitor the situation, but within a month, Stacy had lost so much weight she was in trouble, with severe dehydration and changes in her heart rhythm.

Gloria recalls how hard it was to watch her daughter deteriorate: "The doctor believed Stacy when she said everything was fine, even though she'd lost ten pounds at that first visit. He was totally unconcerned — in fact I think he wondered what was wrong with me for bringing her in. But she's short, so ten pounds was a lot, and that quickly became fifteen, and then twenty."

By the point of extreme weight loss (15 percent under Ideal Body Weight), which often was the point where insurance companies would authorize medical action, a child was often seriously ill. Luckily, the doctor was able to step in before a crisis occurred because Stacy admitted she was struggling with her eating and needed help.

Now It Will Get Better

Like most parents, the Goodes believed that once Stacy's problem was identified, she would quickly be treated and recover. In contrast to the long period of waiting to see if there really was something wrong, they felt sure that doctors would have a ready answer for them after "Anorexia Nervosa" was diagnosed. Their hopes were soon dashed, as were those of many other parents at a similar point in the Discovery phase. This father speaks for many: "I thought once we knew for sure that this wasn't just a developmental fluke or some normal fluctuation in her weight there would be a quick recovery, but that isn't what happened."

Parents who made these types of statements equated a diagnosis with the child's willingness to recover, which rarely occurred at the same time. All too often, the eating disorder seemed to get <u>worse</u> after it was recognized, regardless of whether it was anorexia or bulimia. One father recalls with great bitterness that having a diagnosis seemed to give his daughter "permission" to binge and purge regularly because her secret was now out in the open.

In a small number of cases, diagnosis did set a child on the road to recovery. While I did not specifically ask how long the Discovery phase lasted for these children, one parent offered that his son's behavior went on for years before being diagnosed through a medical crisis. Even then, the parents were not offered any options. The parents arranged for an appointment at a clinic that worked with children facing similar problems.

"The therapist came in on a Sunday. He resisted going, saying there was nothing wrong, so we told him, 'Fine, if she says there's nothing wrong, we'll stop bugging you.' She spent a long time with him while we waited, and when she came out and said he had agreed to treatment we breathed a sigh of relief."

Although it took several months of hard work after that, the admission of a problem began the recovery process for this young man.

Second Guessing

After diagnosis, many parents (the Goodes included) wondered if they should have gotten help sooner, perhaps by seeking a second or third opinion. They worried they may have said something that spurred on their child's disordered eating, and debated when the problems really began. They saw their child in a new light, and recognized their child had the power to control parental emotions and behavior through the child's eating.

"I felt like I was on a tightrope. My instinct was to make a big deal, and start insisting on this or that, but people warned me not to. I believe that could have turned my daughter away from treatment she finally agreed to, but who knows? Maybe she would have gone sooner."

It seems doubtful that what a parent says or does early on will either stop or encourage an eating disorder. I've received a striking number of e-mails and letters from girls who say their parents never knew about (or at least never acknowledged) their anorexia or bulimia, even when the situation was obvious. These young women later went on to seek treatment on their own, or continued to suffer alone, with struggles that sounded as acute as many girls with very involved parents.

Many parenting decisions get made on instinct. If you are a parent with a concern about your child remember that you have lived with your child for many years. You have seen him or her over a lifetime, sick, healthy, sad, and happy.

Trust your ability to know when something is not right.

RESOURCES

Some additional resources on interventions can be found in much of the literature and websites devoted to substance abuse:

http://alcoholism.about.com/cs/info2/a/aa100897.htm
Although written for persons with alcohol abuse, this two part article covers key principles and concerns related to an intervention.

How to Help Someone Who Doesn't Want Help by Dr. Vernon Johnson (Published in 1986 by Hazelden) provides a guide for interventions.

Love First by Jeff and Debra Jay (Published in 2000 by Hazelden Publishing). Another discussion of how to plan an intervention.

4
Tell Me Why

৵৽৽

"BEFORE ALL THIS HAPPENED, I USED TO FEEL GOOD ABOUT MYSELF, AND TO LOOK AT MY TWO OLDER DAUGHTERS AND FEEL PROUD OF MY PARENTING. NOW ALL I CAN DO IS ASK 'WHY?' WHAT DID I DO WRONG?" MOTHER OF A GIRL DIAGNOSED WITH BULIMIA AS A COLLEGE SOPHOMORE

Even now, Ron can't understand why his oldest daughter Sara developed anorexia during her first year of college. Although Sara recovered after three years of treatment and is now married and enjoying her life, he remains puzzled. Was he was too strict a father? Was there some sign of disordered eating he missed during what he thought was a normal childhood?

Ron's wife May also thinks back on the time in high school when a boy made fun of Sara's "cow hips." She remembers that Sara's best friend had a one year struggle with anorexia when they were both in ninth grade, but neither of those events seems significant enough to predict all that happened later.

It was easy for Ron and May to retrace incidents in Sara's childhood that only took on significance after she developed an eating disorder. The longer they thought, the more evidence accumulated.

Ever since her pregnancy with Zac, Sara's younger brother, May had battled to lose an extra twenty pounds. Had her comments about fattening food somehow influenced Sara? In high school, she and Sara had gone on diets together, coaching each other through exercise and meal regimens designed to help them lose weight. Was this to blame?

Ron, on the other hand, had always been extremely thin. He could eat large amounts of food without gaining an ounce, but rarely craved desserts, which his children and wife loved. Sara, in particular, seemed to have a sweet tooth. During one family therapy session, Ron suddenly remembered an incident when Sara had eaten most of the chocolate cake left over from her tenth birthday party. He had chastised her, and dumped the remaining cake in the garbage. In tears, he admitted to telling his daughter if she wanted cake so much, she could eat it out of the garbage, because that's what it was.

Sara herself didn't even remember many of these experiences, and didn't place any importance on them. She said she wasn't sure why she became bulimic, but thought in part it was due to dating a wrestler in high school who used vomiting for weight control. Confronted with gaining the "freshman fifteen" at college she had thought it an easy way to control her weight.

Despite the circumstances of any individual child (younger, older, male, female, intact family or not, bulimia or anorexia) parents like Ron and May uniformly blamed themselves for "causing" the eating disorder. Few parents discussed the lack of awareness their children may have had about how dangerous eating disorders can be, or the influence of the American "thin is better" mindset.

This following story, different in extremes from Sara's, resulted in almost the same parent response:

Norma's only son Jim developed bulimia in his junior year of high school. She, too, searched for a reason why. Jim had been chubby in middle school, so perhaps he was responding to the teasing of his classmates. His father lived on the other side of the country but had visitation with Jim in the summer and on holidays. His father was a bit overweight, and tended to use food as a reward when Jim was with him.

As Jim's weight dropped and he admitted he had bulimia, Norma sought out a psychologist to help her deal with her fears and guilt. Was she to blame? Should she have worked harder to find a male role model for Jim who might have involved him in sports? Had she inadvertently used food to comfort Jim when she should have been encouraging him to avoid sweets or snacking?

The Faulty Family Stereotype

Conventional wisdom suggests that there is a certain type of family that may provide fertile breeding ground for eating disorders.

Dr. James Lock of Brown University says: "Historically, many therapists have seen families as pathological and interfacing with the adolescent's ability to develop a sense of self. Thus, clinicians have blamed families, excluded them from treatment, and instead focused on the individual relationship of patient and therapist as the incubus for recovery." [1]

Many if not most of the books about anorexia offer a description of parents as rigid, controlling, perfectionist, over engaged, weight conscious, or weight obsessed. There are supposed to be problems with over engagement with children, and dysfunctional communication patterns. The labels go on and on, encompassing parents who push their children to be high achievers or ridicule their children for shortcomings. I was shocked to discover an article published through my own university's research magazine that discusses "smothering mothering" and other family problems in young women (but not men) with eating disorders! [2]

What may be just as surprising are the methods many experts use to come to their conclusions. Most clinicians (especially the ones who write books on the topics of families and eating disorders) base their opinions about parents on what patients told them. One father recalls that he was shocked to hear the many labels his daughter's therapist had attached to him before he and the counselor had even met. Most often, young women who are ill enough (and therefore malnourished enough) to be in treatment are not the best source of accurate information.

Researchers who write scholarly articles on the type of families associated with anorexia or bulimia often collect their data from "convenient" samples of young women with eating disorders. Unlike rigorous clinical trials where subjects are carefully selected, those who are most readily available are studied, and with anorexia or bulimia this means those patients who are on the verge (or actually in the middle) of hospitalization and therefore acutely ill. Obviously, the reliability of information obtained from a malnourished young woman in the midst of a medical crisis should be suspect.

(Note: As of this writing I could not find any information specific to families of boys who develop eating disorders.)

Counterpoint

In contrast, a recent article by psychologist Shan Guisinger asserts that families are not at all to blame for eating disorders.[3] After years of clinical practice and research, Dr. Guisinger failed to find commonalities among the families of the patients she was treating. This led to a study that suggests a primitive biological drive regulating starvation behaviors explains far more about anorexia than the behavior of mothers and fathers.

KEY POINTS OF GUISINGER'S STUDY:
- "Anorexic response" is part of a biologic drive that gets turned on by starvation
- The brain adapts to levels of body fat
- Hyperactivity and a sense of purpose are part of the body's response to starvation
- Treatments focused on family dysfunction are misguided

Despite evidence like Guisinger's and newer work on genetic causes of eating disorders, every parent questions why his or her child has developed an eating disorder, and how he or she might have caused or treated it. That questioning often leads to an intense search for answers and explanations that might lead to a "cure."

Straight to the Source

Knowing all this, I was curious to hear what parents had to say about their role in their children's lives, and how they thought their families had functioned <u>before</u> the eating disorder.

(I couldn't find anyone who had actually asked for this kind of input from parents.)

My question was: "Tell me what life was like for you and your child before the anorexia or bulimia." Of course, in most cases moms and dads were looking back several years, so what they told me was probably based on their more intense memories. Still, their responses didn't match what I might have expected based on the books and articles I had read.

While a few mothers and one father admitted they dieted from time to time, like May, there was no excessive focus on food intake or weight for either the parents or children. In two cases, there were other female relatives who had eating disorders, but no one in the immediate family.

In fact, families sounded like any cross section of families across the country might: the majority of parents had been married for a long time, but two were in the early stages of a second marriage. A handful of single parents [divorced or widowed] were also represented in my interviews.

In some cases both parents worked outside the home, while in others they did not. There was a mix of professional and blue collar occupations.

Children were described before their illnesses in a range of ways. Some were portrayed as eager to please and overachieving, others as "average teenagers," and still others as emotional or even a bit challenging. Some were picky eaters, others were not. A few had experienced depression, but most had never seen the inside of a therapist's or guidance counselor's office.

As I reviewed my records again and again, I struggled to find some kind of pattern that captured all families, but the only compelling finding was the diversity in the childhoods of these sons and daughters. Ultimately, it was impossible to identify pre-illness behaviors that suggested an inclination or potential to become eating disordered. None were described as having an excessive focus on food, dieting, or their bodies.

The only commonality across families I could find was involvement in sports. At one time or another, many sons and daughters participated in an organized athletic program — but what child doesn't these days?

This doesn't mean families were trouble-free, or functioned perfectly, although in many cases, before the eating disorder occurred the parents described relationships with their children that sounded pretty typical. If I randomly stopped dozens of people in my local shopping mall and asked the same questions, I suspect I would hear the same kind of responses. Holidays, vacations, and weekends were spent in activities with children, extended family was often an integral part of life, and spiritual development was an important value.

A link between abuse and eating disorders was found in two families. In one case, a girl had a history of sexual abuse that hadn't been previously disclosed. In another, a boy was abused in childhood by using food as a reward and punishment. None of the other families reported this connection, but I didn't specifically ask about it.

Obviously, the reports and family history I received from these mothers and fathers may have been distorted or misreported. Out of grief or guilt, stories might have been skewed or even deliberately changed, just as patients in the throes of an eating disorder may not accurately express their thoughts and memories. Regardless, the perceptions of parents of children with eating disorders should be taken as genuine and no less accurate than those of any other parent with a chronically ill child.

The Search Continues

Understanding "why" is an important but almost impossible dilemma for parents. During the acute phase of their daughter's anorexia, Ron and Mary spent hours either searching the Internet for information or combing through the details of Sara's childhood to find evidence that they or someone else had somehow made a critical mistake that led to her eating problems. Secretly, Mary feared that if she didn't come to understand why Sara had become bulimic during the transition time of leaving home, she might relapse when other life changing events (like pregnancy) occurred.

Norma also examined every age and stage of Jim's life. She and his father had divorced when Jim was four, and although Norma's father had tried to step in and provide a male presence, perhaps it hadn't been enough. Jim had complained about some incidents which occurred in the cafeteria during seventh grade — had she taken his comments too lightly? Were the incidents she considered teasing really serious emotional abuse?

Other parents discuss the issue of "why?"

"They tell you it's not your fault but you think, 'Was it because I didn't let her have a bunch of cookies as a kid?'"

"I kind of think we were just one of the inevitable parents that had a daughter with an eating disorder, and we were definitely not going to cure it nor was any doctor or outpatient level gonna fix it either."

"We may never know and she may never know. So you just have to work with the here and now and not worry about what caused it. Just focus on how you can help."

"As much as we've been through there were no big significant family problems or anything like that. As a matter of fact, I thought I had some pretty darn easy children."

As Norma and May and Ron reached out to their circle of friends, they sometimes felt as if other moms and dads agreed there must be something wrong with the parenting Sara and Jim had received. Mary described parents who swiftly denied ever having similar problems with any of their children, conveying (in her opinion) a belief that they thought eating disorders "just couldn't happen" to them. The notion that families have the ability to protect or prevent eating disorders was echoed in a letter I received from a woman whose daughter developed anorexia: "We do not have the kind of home where these things happen." These impressions and failure to identify a "reason" for anorexia or bulimia intensified feelings of guilt and failure.

The need for explanation seems to be part of human nature. From my previous books, clinical work, and personal experience I know that part of the coping process involves understanding the "whys" of life, but with eating disorders (and many other situations) there simply are no clear cut answers. As a therapist commented to me: "Parenting is a crap shoot. While we tend to pat ourselves on the back if our kids turn out okay, in reality it's a lot of luck. Sometimes all the right pieces are in place and all the 'rules' followed and still a child struggles horribly. It could be genetics, it could be peers, it could be the way the planets were aligned at that particular moment. No one really knows."

The Expert Answer — Or Not

"Why?" was often one of the first questions posed to health care professionals, where parents turned next for an explanation. Believing that doctors or therapists could solve (and therefore cure) the mystery of a son or daughter's eating disorder, Ron, Mary, and Norma took their children for a clinic visit, expecting to leave with all of their questions answered.

When this didn't happen (and it rarely if ever does), Ron's disappointment with their family doctor and Norma's anger at the therapist her friends suggested was overwhelming. In the weeks that followed the initial visits, Sara and Jim's parents consulted several other professionals in an attempt to find help.

These parents are typical of the ones I talked to in their belief that a single solution to their child's eating disorder could be identified and quickly applied. Although they would later realize how unrealistic their expectations were, at the time of their first contact with the health care system they brought with them a desperate need to find some way, any way, to resolve their child's eating disorder. This drive dominated all other thoughts.

Compounding the parents' naiveté was the inability of professionals, no matter how many years of experience in eating disorders they had, to explain why. Some doctors failed to even recognize what. Even more disturbing was being confronted with professionals who treated parents as peripheral, or, worse yet, judged them. Many mothers felt as if therapists and physicians they encountered acted as if they believed in a type of "anorexigenic" mother, much as psychiatrists of the last century believed mothers of children with schizophrenia were the cause of the illness, labeling them "schizophrenagenic." That theory was abandoned when studies on genetics provided stronger support for the apparent family connection. There are still debates about the true cause of schizophrenia.[4]

"One of the therapists actually commented on how petite I was and said that I must watch my weight!" a mother exclaimed indignantly, noting that in any other situation such a remark wouldn't have been tolerated. Other moms found that therapy often focused on their relationship with their ill children, rather than on how the entire family interacted.

"It was like, okay, your husband can't come in for family therapy, but you be here anyway," the wife of a busy doctor shared. Repeatedly, she attended multiple sessions of therapy where her parenting rather than that of the absent father was critiqued.

Another mother had similar feelings about family therapy, renaming it "mother bashing." "Yeah, that's when they all get to trash me," she said, citing examples of sessions where both her daughter, who had bulimia, and her son, who did not have an eating disorder, were encouraged to "verbalize" their dissatisfaction with her. All of these experiences reinforced the cycle of self blame mothers were already caught up in.

Is there a single causative factor for eating disorders? In reality, experts will tell you (as do some of those on the sites listed below) that the causes are multiple. I received this explanation early on, too, when a psychiatrist drew a circle divided into thirds, which represented family, society, and the traits of the individual child. Although he told me that all factors in combination influenced the development of eating disorders, like most of the parents I interviewed, it might as well have been a circle with my name inside it.

In the end, the "why" of eating disorders may not matter that much. One father discovered that when the focus of treatment shifted away from family history and toward his daughter's current eating patterns, she began to recover. Nonetheless, it seems to be an almost inevitable and perhaps necessary part of initial coping. Why? Despite plenty of conjectures, not one parent I talked with ever had a definite answer, even after years of recovery.

RESOURCES

These websites are just a smattering of the many that offer summaries of opinions from "experts" but no conclusive evidence of a single "cause" of eating disorders:

http://www.anred.com/causes.html
http://www.hec.ohio-state.edu/bitf/etiology.htm
http://www.ucdmc.ucdavis.edu/ucdhs/health/a/
49EatingDisorders/doc49causes.html

Each of these sites discuss multiple internal and external factors that influence the development of eating disorders, placing more or less credibility on biological, social, or psychological aspects.

http://web4health.info/en/answers/ed-causes-overview.htm
Contains several papers authored by different experts who offer an equally diverse range of opinions on psychological, social, and family influences.

http://web4health.info/en/answers/ed-causes-addictive.htm
Discusses similarities between addictions and eating disorders.

CHAPTER FOUR FOOTNOTES

[1] http://www.childresearch.net/CYBRARY/NEWS/200104.HTM
An issue of The Brown University Child and Adolescent Behavior
Letter by James Lock, MD, PhD.

[2] Read online at http://www.rps.psu.edu/jan99/starving.html.

[3] http://www.boston.com/yourlife/health/fitness/articles/2003/12/30/
the_ancestry_of_anorexia/.

[4] See http://www.mental-health-today.com/sphra/schiz.htm.

5
Everything Falls Apart

꙰

"FOR THE FIRST TIME, I COULDN'T CONTROL THE
CIRCUMSTANCES. TO THIS POINT, MY DAUGHTER AND I HAD
BEEN CLOSE, THERE WERE NO FAMILY PROBLEMS, AND I'D
BEEN HAPPILY MARRIED FOR TWENTY-FIVE YEARS.
SUDDENLY, THAT WAS ALL GONE." MOTHER, *ON HOW SHE
REACTED TO THE DIAGNOSIS*

When Adam went off to college his parents thought he
had successfully "left the nest." His mother Ann, a
social worker, and his father Bill, an engineer, believed he
was doing well at school since they got glowing reports each
time they talked to him. They were amazed when Adam came
home on Thanksgiving break and they barely recognized him.
In the span of three months, their son's build had gone from
average to emaciated. Even Adam's younger brothers asked
Ann what was wrong with him.

As a social worker, Ann lost no time in confronting her
son, and demanding to know what was going on. She and Bill
had already decided they would not allow Adam to return to
school unless he agreed to seek treatment. In many ways, Ann
was angry because she suspected Adam had been binging and
purging during his senior year of high school to keep his weight
in control. Again and again she had questioned him about his

food behaviors, but he staunchly denied any problems. Now, seeing him after so many months away, she realized she had been right, and that he had repeatedly deceived her. "What you have to realize, is they will lie to you again and again," she says. "And they don't even see it as dishonest, I really believe that. Adam certainly didn't. He thought I was overreacting."

Ann's background as a social worker positioned her to know a bit about eating disorders, and her high school suspicions had led her to talk about bulimia with Stan, a colleague and fellow therapist. Stan told her that some of the power of eating disorders often comes from keeping the problem a secret, and expressed hope for Adam's willingness to seek treatment and recovery.

Despite her ability to calmly discuss her son's past deception and her nagging suspicion that Adam was bulimic, Ann nonetheless dreaded hearing the truth. Adam agreed to see a therapist who specialized in eating disorders, who invited Bill and Ann to join them at the end of the intake interview. Crammed into a small office, they learned just how serious Adam's problem was: he had lost an extreme amount of weight, and was binging, purging, and restricting his intake so regularly it scared him.

The therapist told them it was actually fortunate that Adam, technically an adult, consented to allow his parents into the session, but Ann didn't feel fortunate. She felt devastated.

Bill was hurt, too. "I mean, I just couldn't believe he would do this. We would have been behind him 100 percent if he had come to us and asked for help, but instead he ended up in a condition where I was worried he would die."

Life Changes

When confronted with a diagnosis that in many ways ended family life as parents knew it, there were a variety of responses. In one situation, a husband was completely baffled by his daughter's eating disorder, and handled her with "kid gloves" from the point of diagnosis on, leaving his wife to take care of most of the treatment activities. His wife, in turn, became quickly overwhelmed after her shock wore off. She said: "From that moment [diagnosis] on, it became my obsession. If I was at work, I would make phone calls related to her. If I was at home, I was checking on her or trying to come up with new ideas on how to help her. I could never get away from it. Even when I finally fell asleep, I would dream about her."

Another mom, who is a nurse, flashed back to her younger years when she received her daughter's diagnosis: "I had a patient with anorexia when I was first in nursing school, and remember thinking how that kind of thing would never happen to anyone close to me. It almost came back to haunt me."

Ann understands these feelings. She said: "Here I am, this social work person who's supposed to be an expert at helping other parents figure out how to take care of their kids, and I couldn't even do it for Adam. I failed him in some essential way, and it really hurt."

The Bulimia Stigma

When parents received a diagnosis of their children's eating disorder, it seemed that bulimia evoked a greater sense of embarrassment and dismay than anorexia, a perception that stayed with me throughout discussions of other aspects of caregiving. I base this impression on the tone of voice parents had when describing bulimic behaviors (hushed and apologetic) and what they said. Many times, the behavior of a bulimic child was referred to obliquely as "the other thing," and when signs and symptoms seemed more indicative of bulimia, the parent still referred to it as anorexia. (Several online articles by therapists suggest the sense of shame is indeed greater with bulimia for multiple reasons. Search online for "bulimia stigma" to learn more.)

Again, a disclaimer. Even experts admit there is overlap between anorexia and bulimia, and sometimes the diagnosis doesn't fit either illness, but falls into a third area labeled ED-NOS (eating disorder not otherwise specified). A summary of the key criteria for eating disorders in the *Diagnostic Standards Manual* (DSM) (the gold standard of psychiatry) can be found on page 83.

That being said, in contrast to parents who talked in a straightforward way about anorexia, these were the kinds of comments parents made about their initial response to a diagnosis of bulimia.

"So then, she admitted to the doctor that she, uh, she was...what do you call it, purging? Throwing up all her food? And we just couldn't understand why anyone would do that."

"It was disgusting to find vomit in the toilet, and to realize what she was doing. But when it all came out and she told the doctor, I was ashamed to think of all that food she wasted."

"Suddenly I understood it all, her running to the bathroom after we ate, the quantity of food she could eat in one sitting, the reason for our plumbing constantly backing up. The details of it were revolting, but whatever was inside her driving this upset me even more."

A few children with bulimia were also cutters. A simple explanation of cutting is that a person uses a sharp object for self injury — not as a suicidal gesture so much as an expression of distress or a coping mechanism. When parents discovered cutting, they again entered the cycle of fear and self blame. Seeing behaviors which were so obvious and destructive was very difficult to bear.

When she learned of her daughter's cutting one mother described her worry over what each new day would hold, and wondered how she would survive the constant anxiety: "Would she cut herself deeply enough to do real harm? Would she rupture something while vomiting?"

In some ways, this mom found the pre-diagnosis state of uncertainty easier to cope with because then there was still a chance nothing was seriously wrong.

Bothered, Blamed, and Bereaved

The initial confusion and concern of Discovery that eventually led to a diagnosis elicited new emotions in parents. The confirmation that their children did indeed have anorexia or bulimia sometimes led to anger. Fathers in particular seemed to respond this way:

"We couldn't understand why he was doing it. You want only the best for your children, and you want to help them, and you want to guide them. And when you go through something like this, we were doing all the wrong things I think at first. I couldn't understand it, I was saying it would quit if you'd just start eating again."

"We didn't know what it was all about, and we were hurt and we were afraid, and that fear propelled us in the wrong direction. We tried to control, with a lot of shouting and anger, and that made it worse."

A mother shared: "For a long time I felt sick to my stomach, and then I began to get mad. I kept trying to talk to my son in a caring manner. It's very hard for me not to blame myself for this."

Along with the diagnosis, a few parents were told the treatment that would be required to help their children was lengthy, intense, and often complicated. This evoked a sense of further dismay: "I hated when they told me in the beginning to be prepared for the long haul. But you can't think: one week and it's under wraps!"

For those who weren't told what to expect, a belief that doctors and therapists would have a quick fix for their children persisted. Later, they realized that a combination of failure to communicate and lack of information created unrealistic expectations that colored their relationships from the start, as evidenced by these statements:

"They never told me this would likely be years of treatment rather than months. I think if I had known this, it would have changed my attitude from the beginning. I would have accepted that I couldn't 'fix' her, and I wouldn't have expected them to either."

"The pediatrician gave me some outdated brochure on mental health, and I wondered why. It made no sense to me that she would be seeing a medical doctor if her problem was psychological."

"I had lots of questions, as you can imagine, but the therapist told me not to seek so much information, and to just place my trust in the doctors and her. But they weren't at home with us dealing with the behaviors every day. I needed down to earth advice on how to respond to my child."

"I think they should arrange for some kind of parent advocate who has the time to sit with you, even if it's just an hour, and explain what might happen. I know there aren't any answers, but there is information that helps, and it doesn't come from doctors or nurses."

In addition to anger, there seemed to be other gender-based differences. Mothers were quicker to blame themselves for the eating disorder, and also seemed to instantly assume the role of primary caregiver. On learning the diagnosis, most began to immediately form a strategy on how to help their children. Fathers were no less concerned, but many expressed "solution-oriented" thoughts that involved suggestions that their children should just change the behavior and move on.

Diagnosis brought with it sorrow and self blame, frustration with "experts," and a deep sense of grieving. Even if the pre-diagnosis period had been long or the suspicions almost a certainty, the confirmation that a son or daughter really was seriously ill felt like a hard physical blow. It hurt on impact and stayed tender for a long time after.

DIAGNOSING ANOREXIA AND BULIMIA

HERE IS A SUMMARY OF THE BASIC CRITERIA FOR DIAGNOSING ANOREXIA AND BULIMIA, BASED ON THE *DIAGNOSTIC STANDARDS MANUAL*, A GUIDE USED BY CLINICIANS TO ESTABLISH MENTAL HEALTH DISORDERS. (AMERICAN PSYCHIATRIC ASSOCIATION. *DIAGNOSTIC AND STATISTICAL MANUAL OF MENTAL DISORDERS, 4TH ED (DSM-IV)*. WASHINGTON, DC: AMERICAN PSYCHIATRIC ASSOCIATION; 1994). IF YOU WOULD LIKE TO SEE AN INFORMATIVE POWER POINT PRESENTATION ON THESE CRITERIA, VISIT HTTP://MEDINFO.UFL.EDU/YEAR1/HUMBEHAV/POWERPOINT%20FILES/EATING%20DISORDERS-MS1-2004.PPT

ANOREXIA NERVOSA
- UNREASONABLE FEAR OF WEIGHT GAIN
- WEIGHT THAT IS BELOW 85% OF IDEAL BODY WEIGHT
- DISTORTED BODY IMAGE (PERCEPTION OF BEING "FAT" DESPITE WEIGHT)
- DENIAL THAT WEIGHT IS LOW ENOUGH TO CAUSE CONCERN
- MISSING THREE OR MORE CONSECUTIVE MENSTRUAL PERIODS

DIFFERENT TYPES OF ANOREXIA ARE CLASSIFIED AS **RESTRICTING** (LIMITING INTAKE) OR **BINGE/PURGE** (ALL OF THE ABOVE SYMPTOMS, AND BINGING — CONSUMING LARGE QUANTITIES OF FOOD IN A SHORT TIME AND FEELING NO CONTROL OVER FOOD INTAKE. PURGING — VOMITING FOOD OR TAKING LAXATIVES)

BULIMIA NERVOSA
- "BINGE" EATING
- EXCESSIVE USE OF BEHAVIORS INTENDED TO CONTROL WEIGHT IN ADDITION TO PURGING: EXERCISE, LAXATIVES, DIURETICS (ELIMINATING FLUID), OR RESTRICTING
- THESE BEHAVIORS OCCUR TWICE/WEEK FOR LONGER THAN 3 MONTHS
- THINKS OF HIM OR HERSELF IN TERMS OF WEIGHT

DIFFERENT TYPES OF BULIMIA ARE CLASSIFIED AS **PURGING** (USING VOMITING, LAXATIVES, OR DIURETICS) VERSUS **NONPURGING** (USING OTHER BEHAVIORS)

IF A CHILD HAS SOME BUT NOT ALL OF THESE BEHAVIORS, HE OR SHE MAY BE CLASSIFIED AS ED-NOS (EATING DISORDER NOT OTHERWISE SPECIFIED). COMPULSIVE OVEREATING IS AN EXAMPLE OF ED-NOS.

NOTE: IN ADDITION TO A PSYCHIATRIC DIAGNOSIS, YOUR CHILD MAY HAVE MEDICAL DIAGNOSES RELATED TO MALNUTRITION OR LOW BODY WEIGHT.

RESOURCES

For more information:

http://www.d.umn.edu/hlthserv/counseling/ED/definitions_eating.html
A quiz on eating disorders that gives more specific descriptions of behaviors.

http://www.iamcurly.com/ednos.html
Offers a very good description of ED-NOS behaviors.

http://www.rainbowpediatrics.net/faq/15.2.html
Contains DSM criteria for eating disorders.

Section Two

৵৵

A Team of Your Own: Finding, Keeping, and Paying for Treatment

6
The Health Care Team:
Is It Really?

༈

"DON'T FOOL YOURSELF. IT'S NOT A TEAM AND WE'RE NOT PART OF IT." *A FATHER, ASKED ABOUT HIS EXPERIENCE WITH THE HEALTH CARE TEAM TREATING HIS DAUGHTER*

Sandy and Lon's fourteen-year-old son Bill swings between anorexia and bulimia, sometimes restricting his intake until he loses a drastic amount of weight, and other times binging and purging several times a day. Bill's eating behaviors are so extreme that he has suffered medical consequences: dehydration, intestinal problems, and cardiac arrhythmias have led to several hospitalizations.

Despite their efforts to find inpatient programs that accept boys, Sandy and Lon have ended up having to take care of Bill at home, with the help of several health care professionals. At one point, a feeding tube was inserted in Bill's stomach to help provide much needed nutrition, but even then there seemed to be no program that would accept him as an inpatient so he could receive therapy for his eating disorder.

Sandy and Lon share in the care of Bill, who is seen by several different health care providers on a regular basis. Sandy has made it her job to become informed about anorexia and bulimia, regularly searching the Internet for research studies and information from other parents that may help her son. She recognizes she is the one who will coordinate Bill's care by working with the many different health care professionals who treat him. On a regular basis, she contacts each of them with updates on his condition.

Lon is the back-up person. He takes over when he comes home from work and finds his wife stressed by a day alone with Bill, and several times he has used personal days to drive Bill to doctor and therapist appointments. He admits the different specialists involved in his son's care and the role they each play is confusing to him. Although he goes to as many of his son's appointments as he can, he lets Sandy do the talking for both of them, and defers to her in most medical decisions that need to be made.

"She could work as a nurse by this point," he says.

In therapy sessions, however, the roles reverse and it is Lon who is the primary contact with Bill's therapist, Louise. Although most of the time Louise sees Bill alone, on the few occasions when Lon and Sandy were asked to participate, it was difficult. Sandy felt "attacked" by Louise, and Lon, sensing this, became defensive of his wife. Since Bill likes Louise and feels he works well with her, Lon has continued taking Bill to see her while Sandy stays home for some much needed "alone time."

RESOURCES FOR BOYS

These websites contain information on treatment for boys:
http://www.afterthediet.com/Weltzin — Residential%20Males.htm
http://www.something-fishy.org/treatment/md.php

The Yin and Yang of Eating Disorders

Unlike other forms of mental illness, eating disorders cause serious problems that can affect both physical and mental health. The medical aspects of an eating disorder relate to nutrition. Any acute or prolonged nutritional imbalance resulting from lack of food, excess food, or repeated vomiting can lead to serious problems related to the function of the stomach, kidneys, bones, brain, and heart. For example, two parents had daughters who required hospitalization and needed complete bed rest for several days because they were so nutritionally compromised. The possibility of serious compromise to health and even death is always present with bulimia and anorexia, which some experts feel are the most fatal of all psychiatric disorders.

COMPLICATIONS AND MORTALITY RATES

http://www.pbs.org/perfectillusions/help/seeking_facts.html
Offers information on eating disorder complications and mortality rates for anorexia and bulimia.

http://www.state.sc.us/dmh/anorexia/statistics.htm
More specific statistics on mortality rates.

http://www.netdoctor.co.uk/diseases/facts/anorexianervosa.htm
Medical doctors discuss complications that can occur with anorexia or bulimia.

http://river-centre.org/PhysicalComp.html
A gritty and detailed medical description of physical complications associated with eating disorders and mortality.

As is common, for Bill the psychological aspects of eating disorders manifested as a disruption of thought processes about food and perceptions of his body. Bill was obsessed with food, and had many rules and rituals that prevented him from taking in an adequate number of calories. Without food, malnutrition resulted, impairing the ability of his brain to work normally. This cycle of his altered thought processes and abnormal food behaviors led to continued nutritional imbalance. Other emotional problems that may or may not be related to malnutrition (depression and borderline personality disorder, to give two examples) occur so often with eating disorders, some feel they may actually be part of the disease.

As physical and psychological health deteriorates, the ability to engage in normal activities of daily life and connect in meaningful ways with other people seems to fall apart, too. Sandy found this to be true of Bill. He dropped his friends and lost interest in relationships with peers, as did many other children whose parents noticed that their son or daughter's food focus crowded out any attention previously given to peers.

One mother said: "My daughter began to turn away from all her friends, who were trying to help her. She was convinced they were envious of her weight, which was why they urged her to eat. Eventually, they got tired of hanging around with a girl who was fixated on food and who was too weak to do any of the things they used to enjoy together."

The mental and physical aspects of eating disorders have a way of interacting with and compounding each other, as they did with Bill. Both aspects of the disease need to be treated before improvement will occur: if only medical needs are focused on, eating disordered thought patterns will persist, and vice versa. This means a number of health care professionals are needed to address the multiple issues related to anorexia and bulimia.

A Cast of Care Providers

Given the complex nature of eating disorders, when a child is as ill as Bill, parents like Sandy and Lon end up interacting with and coordinating care between a treatment team of professionals, each with a different and important role. Insurance companies are often focused on who is providing care, and may provide or withhold reimbursement accordingly.

Being an informed consumer means that you, the caregiver, and your child need to understand the credentials and roles of anyone involved in your child's treatment. Even if a person seems to be experienced or pleasant, if that person has not been properly licensed and trained, the therapeutic relationship may fail. Again and again, parents regretted not acting in a more empowered role to learn about the professionals treating their children and not being assertive in communicating their feelings about the care provided.

You may already be an experienced "health care consumer." If you're not, or you need an overview of the "key players" who often became part of the eating disorder treatment team, here is a simplified breakdown.

Medical Care

Most but not all of the parents interviewed had children whose eating disorder was treated medically. Medical care included things like regular weigh-ins on a standardized hospital scale, blood work to check on nutritional status, and prescription of various medications. If a patient required hospital admission or more intensive therapies, medical care might include intravenous (IV) fluids and/or nasogastric (NG) or other feeding tubes, sometimes provided on an outpatient (living at home) basis. At other times, these treatments were part of an admission to the hospital so a child's status could be more closely monitored.

To obtain these kinds of services, patients had to see a licensed medical or osteopathic doctor (MD or DO) or a nurse practitioner. In addition to these choices for a primary care provider, there were also physicians and nurse practitioners who had specialties that might lead them to become involved in a child's care. For example, if there were problems with a child's stomach, a gastrointestinal specialist might be consulted. If an inpatient stay in the hospital was required, there could be a "hospitalist," a physician who worked primarily in the hospital to take care of all children on the pediatric service.

Most often, the parents I spoke with first sought out a pediatrician (a medical doctor (MD) or doctor of osteopathy (DO) specialized in the care of children up to the age of 18) to evaluate their sons or daughters. At least four parents found that the pediatricians they took their children to either knew little about eating disorders or did not make a prompt diagnosis. "We went to several different doctors, starting with our family pediatrician, and they all missed the boat completely," said one mother.

Another parent recalled selecting a female pediatrician who had recently opened her practice because he thought she might be knowledgeable about eating disorders. His daughter ended up seeing her and two other doctors before anorexia was diagnosed.

In addition to pediatricians, physicians who practiced in family medicine, internal medicine, and primary care were sought out as an initial point of contact. When available, pediatricians board certified in adolescent medicine were suggested as the first professional to approach.

In one case, a nurse practitioner who worked with a physician was actually the one who helped the family. A father describes it this way: "Thank God there was a nurse practitioner there who had just finished her training in [city]. She took us aside and gave us a referral to a clinic where she trained, and that finally got us on the right track."

Unlike registered nurses (RNs) who are found in nearly every doctor's office and clinic setting, some physicians and health care organizations employ nurse practitioners, who have a variety of titles: NP, CRNP, or CNS. All nurse practitioners have graduate training in medicine and often see patients for routine visits in place of a physician. Nurse practitioners are licensed differently in every state, so they may or may not be certified to write out prescriptions and obtain insurance reimbursement. Many perform most of the functions of the MD/DO listed above.

Once families did find a physician and therapist they could work with, their children were often asked to return for regular visits. Most insurance companies don't restrict the number of visits a patient can make to his or her medical doctor given a legitimate illness. The same is rarely true with mental health visits, which often have a cap with insurance programs.

SPECIAL THERAPIES AND TREATMENTS

THERE ARE SPECIAL THERAPIES PHYSICIANS CAN USE TO PROVIDE NUTRITION TO A CHILD QUICKLY. WHILE IT MAY BE INTIMIDATING TO SEE THE EQUIPMENT, THESE TREATMENTS ARE BECOMING MORE COMMONPLACE FOR EATING DISORDERS, AND OFFER REASSURANCE THAT IT WILL BE POSSIBLE TO GET NUTRITION INTO A PERSON WITH ANOREXIA OR BULIMIA.

*INTRAVENOUS THERAPY (IV) IS PRESCRIBED TO PROVIDE ELECTROLYTES, FLUID, CALORIES, VITAMINS, OR OTHER KINDS OF NUTRITION AS WELL AS MEDICATIONS. THE IV FLUID IS INFUSED DIRECTLY INTO A VEIN IN A NUMBER OF DIFFERENT WAYS, DEPENDING ON A CHILD'S NEEDS. SOMETIMES A SIMPLE NEEDLE IS PLACED IN THE HAND OR ARM AND CONNECTED TO THE IV TUBING AND BAG OF FLUID AS NEEDED. AT OTHER TIMES, A LARGER CATHETER IS INSERTED INTO A MAJOR VEIN AND SUTURED IN PLACE.

* A NASOGASTRIC TUBE (NG) IS A FLEXIBLE PLASTIC TUBE THAT GETS INSERTED THROUGH THE NOSE, DOWN THE THROAT, AND INTO THE STOMACH. IT CAN BE USED TO GIVE SPECIAL NUTRITIONAL FEEDINGS AND MEDICATIONS TO PREVENT A CHILD FROM SERIOUS CONSEQUENCES OF MALNUTRITION, AND WILL MOST OFTEN BE DISCONNECTED BETWEEN FEEDINGS.

* A PEG TUBE (PERCUTANEOUS ENDOSCOPIC GASTROTOMY) IS ANOTHER TYPE OF TUBE USED WHEN THERE IS A NEED FOR PROLONGED FEEDINGS OR AN NG TUBE ISN'T TOLERATED. IT IS INSERTED THROUGH THE SKIN AND DIRECTLY INTO THE STOMACH, THEN USED TO PROVIDE SPECIAL LIQUID FOOD SIMILAR TO THE NG TUBE.

BOTH FEEDINGS AND IVS ARE ADMINISTERED FROM A PLASTIC BAG WHICH HANGS ON A POLE ABOUT FIVE FEET HIGH. MANY TIMES, AN ELECTRONIC PUMP IS ATTACHED TO THE POLE TO REGULATE THE FLOW OF FEEDING OR IV FLUID. IF YOU'RE NOT USED TO IT, THE PUMP ALARM CAN SOUND OMINOUS. IT'S A SIGNAL TO STAFF THAT THE LEVEL OF FLUID IN THE IV OR FEEDING BAG IS GETTING LOW.

Based on the severity of the child's eating disorder, visits to the doctor or nurse practitioner occurred several times within a week, every week, or several times a month. Sometimes, the care of a medical doctor was built into an outpatient or partial program, a situation one mom described as "one stop shopping."

"We would take Andrea to the clinic and she would see everyone during her visit: the medical doctor, her therapist, a nutritionist, and then the support group. While she was doing that, my husband and I could attend a support group for families."

Dental Care

Both anorexia and bulimia can affect the integrity of teeth for different reasons. Regular dental care by a dentist who recognizes the possible complications of an eating disorder were important early on, and in one case it was the dentist who actually detected a girl's bulimia. There are a variety of special toothpastes, mouth rinses, and other therapies that can be prescribed to help preserve teeth.

Psychiatric Care

Mental health care can be provided by a host of individuals. Here are just a few of the professional backgrounds of the therapists families in these interviews used:

- Psychiatrist
- Psychiatric nurse practitioner
- Psychologist
- Licensed clinical social worker
- Mental health counselor

- Marriage and family therapists
- Pastoral counselor

As an informed consumer, knowing the general difference between the educational preparation and job description of these individuals will help you find and pay for appropriate care. Sometimes, parents were confused about the qualifications of therapists in particular, tending to assume the professional was always a psychiatrist.

A psychiatrist is a physician, as described above. He or she is an MD/DO who has specialized in psychiatry, and is licensed to and specialized in prescribing medications and laboratory tests specific to psychiatry. He or she may have admitting privileges, which allows the psychiatrist to have a child hospitalized. Most psychiatrists will not provide the medical treatments prescribed in the previous section, but some might. For example, one psychiatrist weighed her patient with each visit.

Psychiatric nurse practitioners, like regular nurse practitioners, can perform many of the same functions as their medical counterparts, including prescribing medications and ordering laboratory tests. While both a psychiatrist and nurse practitioner are qualified to provide psychotherapy in addition to prescribing psychiatric medications, more and more often their role is restricted to the latter given increasing shortages in numbers of professionals.

"The psychiatrist was basically a pill pusher. We'd wait forever in the waiting room, and then see her for fifteen minutes," said one mom, who discovered such visits were necessary in order to continue receiving prescriptions for her child's antidepressant medication. (Some families did have pediatricians or primary care providers who felt comfortable ordering these medications.)

"I had one psychiatrist tell me she simply will not deal with eating disorder patients because it's too frustrating and time consuming," shared one parent, who ended up taking her daughter to a therapist who was a licensed social worker, as did another mom who gave up after trying to make appointments with several different psychiatrists.

Psychologists, social workers, and other mental health counselors provide the bulk of psychotherapy for patients with eating disorders. While psychologists most often have a PhD, in some states a person with a master's degree can be licensed as a psychologist. Psychologists often use a number of psychological tests to access a patient. Your child may be screened for depression, anxiety and other problems along with his or her eating disorder. For more information on psychologists, or to find a psychologist in your area, consult http://www.apa.org or call The American Psychological Association at 1-800-374-2721.

Social workers are licensed and require a graduate degree in order to practice. Since licensing varies from state to state, it's best to check with the National Association of Social Workers website at http://socialworkers.org or call them at 1-800-638-8799.

A number of other therapists are counselors, psychotherapists (as opposed to psychologists), or Licensed Mental Health Counselors (LMHC). These other types of therapists can be checked on the APA website noted earlier, or call your health insurance mental health provider. The National Alliance for Mental Illness (NAMI) is another good resource for this purpose, and can be accessed online at http://www.nami.org or by telephone at 1-800-950-6264.

Any of these individuals can provide therapy on a one-to- one (individual), group, or family basis, but your insurance company may limit or deny visits or reimbursements. It's also helpful to gather information on the therapists you plan to use, and for what purpose. Researching care and recordkeeping are two valuable caregiving skills. You'll find many tools for these purposes in *The Starving Family Workbook.*

Nurses: Registered nurses (RNs) are almost always a part of the health care team. In schools, they are available on a full or part time basis to address the needs of students. In the medical doctor's office they frequently serve as a liaison between the family and physician, and usually are the ones to weigh the child and take vital signs — two activities parents recognize as important. (One mom negotiated with the nurse to check her child's weight and vital signs and only scheduled a visit with the physician if either of these were unstable.)

If a child is inpatient in a hospital or eating disorder center, nurses become "substitute" moms, providing the bulk of the care needed. One mother recalls waking up in the middle of the night and thinking: "I wonder who is there for my daughter right now, and who will comfort her at three A.M. in the morning if she wakes up and is homesick." Most likely, a nurse is the professional available.

Nurses, like physicians, have basic training in both medical and psychological health, but they can also specialize.

Many nurses who work in eating disorder treatment centers (a hybrid of the hospital to be discussed in a later chapter) have backgrounds in mental health care.

Nutritional Counseling

In addition to therapy and medical care, another standard member of the care team is a dietician or nutritionist. (While these terms are often used interchangeably, the education of a nutritionist is not standardized, but a registered dietitian (RD) must have a bachelor's degree in dietetics, nutrition, home economics, food science, or food service management and registration with the American Dietetics Association.) The role of this individual is to help develop a food plan, review caloric intake, and identify strategies for insuring nutritional balance. Most often, nutritionists were helpful to both parents and patients, but two parents whose children worked with nutritionists had differing views on the benefits obtained:

"I found the nutritionist very helpful because she gave me all kinds of ideas: no 'low fat' food items to be kept in the house, what nutrient dense foods to prepare for my daughter, and all that."

"It was ironic that now we would pay for someone to sit and discuss calories with my daughter for an hour. She could easily teach a course on nutrition. She knows the calorie count of every bite of food that goes in her mouth."

When parents worked with several different nutritionists, sometimes the food guidelines provided would change. For example, one professional suggested that parents make the patient responsible for his or her own food preparation and intake, while others advise against this and encourage mothers and fathers to take complete control of their child's food intake. (Resources for finding a nutritionist are located at the end of this chapter.)

The Maudsley Method, a new approach to treating anorexia, advocates that parents be placed in charge of nutrition, and that a child not be allowed to go without food. This method has been suggested to work best with younger children new to anorexia and still dependent on parents.

THE MAUDSLEY METHOD
(NAMED AFTER THE MAUDSLEY HOSPITAL IN LONDON, WHERE IT DEVELOPED)

PHASE ONE: FOOD IS MEDICINE, AND THE FAMILY IS PLACED IN CHARGE OF ADMINISTERING IT USING REWARDS AND CONSEQUENCES (NO PHYSICAL PUNISHMENT OR FORCE FEEDING ALLOWED.) THE EATING DISORDER IS CONSIDERED AN EXTERNAL FORCE CONTROLLING CHILD, AND NEITHER CHILD NOR PARENT IS TO BLAME.

PHASE TWO: AS WEIGHT IMPROVES, THE CHILD GRADUALLY TAKES BACK CONTROL OF FOOD INTAKE, WHILE FAMILY THERAPY CONTINUES TO HELP PARENTS LOOK AT THEIR OWN FOOD BEHAVIORS.

PHASE THREE: FOCUSES ON CHILD ENGAGING IN NORMAL TASKS OF ADOLESCENCE AND HELPING FAMILY TRANSITION INTO RELATIONSHIPS THAT ARE NOT EATING DISORDERED. THIS IS THE FINAL PHASE.

For more information on The Maudsley Method, check:
http://www.childresearch.net/CYBRARY/NEWS/200104.HTM
An issue of The Brown University Child and Adolescent Behavior Letter by James Lock, MD, PhD, on the Maudsley Method.

http://www.aboutourkids.org/aboutour/articles/anorexia_nervosa.html#the
An article from New York University Child Study Center by Katherine Loeb, PhD which discusses the Maudsley Method.

http://www.altrue.net/site/anadweb/content.php?type=1&id=6981
A discussion of the Maudsley Method from ANAD, the National Association for Anorexia Nervosa and Associated Disorders.

http://www.something-fishy.org/reach/treatmenttypes.php#maudsley
Discussion of the Maudsley Method of treatment for eating disorders.

Ground Control

Whether there were few or many health care providers involved in a child's care, parents found themselves taking on the role of "care manager" for their children. To prevent information from getting overlooked or miscommunicated as it was passed around from team member to team member, mothers and fathers kept track of what therapies were prescribed and by whom. As they went from visit to visit with their child, even if there were only two care providers (a physician and a therapist), parents were the ones to make sure each knew what prescriptions were being taken by the child, and which recommendations were in place.

Hear and Obey

Parents were almost always compliant with the suggestions of doctors, therapists, and nutritionists, even when it went against their own intuition. One mother whose daughter is now in recovery reflects back and wonders: "So many times I went against my natural inclinations and listened to what the doctors or therapists told me because I believed they had more experience than me. Not so! I knew my daughter best, and I now question whether following my gut and doing what seemed right to me at the time would have helped her recover faster."

"It's your job to provide the big picture to the doctor and everyone else. You can't depend on anyone else to do it, especially your sick child," said one parent.

This, then, became a tangible role for parents as they interfaced with a multitude of providers focused on treating their children. Different professionals might rotate in and out of the child's life depending on the stage of treatment, but mothers and fathers were a constant. For the 23 hours of the day when daughters or sons weren't receiving services from the health care system families provided care, observing nutritional intake, physical symptoms, mood swings, social relationships, and status in school, suggesting alternatives, and offering various kinds of support. Parents were the ones who could see how a child responded to various therapies, and knew how well (or poorly) he or she was functioning in the home environment. As the glue that held the "health care team" together, mothers and fathers were a source of information and follow-up that enhanced their children's care and enabled professionals work more effectively. Moreover, all parents were grateful to be able to do this, and anything else needed to help their children.

RESOURCES

Resources for locating a nutritionist:
http://www.cdrnet.org/about/index.htm
The Commission on Dietetic Registration.

http://www.findanutritionist.com/p_directory.html
A Directory of Nutritionists.

7
"To the Rescue:" Doctors, Nurses, and Dieticians

৯৯৯

"So then I thought, well, at last, a doctor, now we're getting somewhere." *A mom who brought her daughter to the primary care office after months of suspecting an eating disorder*

"Who am I to question? She's the doctor, right?" *A father who was unsure about a physician's recommendation to hospitalize his daughter.*

Dr. Baker saw Lydia Webb in her office at the beginning of her sophomore year in high school. She had been Lydia's pediatrician for five years, but in the past her visits had been for routine purposes: annual physicals, occasional bronchitis, and a sprained ankle. Now, however, Lydia's mother Trudy called and scheduled an acute visit because she was worried about her daughter's weight loss and changed behavior. Dr. Baker saw Lydia by herself briefly, then invited Trudy to join them.

"Lydia tells me she has been watching her fat intake so her diet will be healthier," she informed Ms. Webb. "Her vital signs are stable, and she's grown an inch, so maybe that's the reason she looks thinner to you."

Relieved, Trudy paid for the visit and drove Lydia home, determined not to focus so much on her daughter's behavior.

As a single mom, she worked full-time as a pharmacist, and spent much of her free time doing things with or for Lydia and her older brother, Sean.

Now Sean was on a scholarship and in his first year of college four hours away. In his absence, maybe she was paying too much attention to normal fluctuations in Lydia's mood and weight.

In the month that followed, Trudy and Lydia began to struggle openly. Each meal was tense, but it wasn't just the food that bothered Trudy. Her daughter looked like she was losing more weight, her skin was extremely pale, and she was always cold, bundling up in a sweatshirt and sweatpants even on warm days. Once, she turned the thermostat to eighty degrees in an attempt to warm herself.

Although she seemed determined to stay on the swim team, Coach Clemmons had expressed concern to Trudy, noting that Lydia was the only girl who didn't eagerly dive in the pool to fetch the candy he threw in as reward for a hard practice. One day shortly after the visit to Dr. Baker, Coach Clemmons called Trudy at work and said he didn't think it was safe for Lydia to come to practices anymore.

That evening, Trudy found a small notebook she recognized on the kitchen counter. Lydia seemed to take it everywhere with her, transferring it from her purse to backpack daily. Trudy thought it was a diary containing her daughter's deepest thoughts, and was about to close it when she stopped short. The notebook was open to a page Lydia had divided neatly into columns that tracked every calorie, fat gram, and carbohydrate she took in — even chewing gum. The daily total at the bottom of the calorie column shocked Trudy so much she leafed through the other pages and saw similar records for the last three weeks, all recorded in Lydia's tiny, precise writing.

When Lydia came downstairs a few minutes later and saw her mother with the open notebook, she exploded.

"Can't I have any privacy? You're nothing but a nosey bitch who doesn't have a life of her own!" she snarled at her mother.

Before Trudy could respond, her daughter flew back up the stairs and refused to leave her bedroom for the rest of the night.

Since their parents divorced three years earlier, Sean and Lydia had routinely spent one weekend a month with their father, who lived two hours away. That weekend, after Lydia returned from her visit with her dad, Norm telephoned Trudy.

"What the hell is going on?" he demanded. "Lydia looks like she's wasting away to nothing. You'd better do something!"

Hanging up the phone, Trudy confronted Lydia again about her appearance and the notebook. She shared Coach Clemmon's concerns, as well as Norm's and her own.

"We're going back to see Dr. Baker as soon as possible," she informed Lydia in conclusion.

The next morning, Trudy called Dr. Baker's office from work and insisted that Lydia needed to be seen that day. The receptionist told Trudy that Mondays were the busiest day of the week, and there were simply no openings with Dr. Baker. Would she see a nurse practitioner instead? Trudy didn't hesitate to say "yes" and asked her boss for the afternoon off.

Mia, the nurse practitioner, saw Lydia early that afternoon. After a few minutes alone with Lydia, she called Trudy in and asked for her observations. She wrote as Trudy talked, and then checked Lydia's blood pressure and pulse, frowning a bit as she did so.

"We're going to get an ECG to check on how your heart is beating," she told Lydia, wheeling a small machine in and sticking the adhesive electrodes to Lydia's chest. Once the test was finished, she tore off a strip of paper and excused herself. A few minutes later, Dr. Baker came in the exam room, looking flustered.

"Lydia, we really need for you to be honest," she said, sitting down so she was on eye level with both Lydia and Trudy. "Tell us what's going on with your eating. Mia says she's concerned that you have an eating disorder, and from her report, I am too."

Lydia's expression was one Trudy recognized from other times when she'd been caught in a lie. As Dr. Baker, Mia, and Trudy listened, she confessed that she had been restricting her intake, and said what had started as an innocent attempt to adopt healthy eating patterns slowly escalated out of control. She ended by defiantly informing the three women that she felt good about her current weight, and thought there were no problems if she could just maintain it.

Mia spoke up. "Lydia, you're about 10 percent below Ideal Body Weight, which is getting to the danger zone. Your heartbeat is irregular, probably because your potassium level is low."

"My heart?" echoed Lydia.

Dr. Baker was grave: "Eating disorders can damage your heart — even cause cardiac arrest. We're going to get some blood work, and Mia has some information on an eating disorder clinic that just opened nearby. You need to be seen by a specialist as soon as possible."

Lydia latched on to the doctor's first words. "You mean my heart could stop completely, and I could die?"

Dr. Baker nodded. "That's why you need someone familiar with eating disorders to see you. It's a serious medical problem that could affect other parts of your body — your bones, your stomach, and your reproductive system. Mia tells me you haven't had a period in three months, but you were regular before that?"

Lydia hung her head, which affirmed Trudy's fears.

After ordering blood work, Mia telephoned the clinic, and spoke directly to the physician in charge, who asked if Trudy could get Lydia to his office before the end of the day. Feeling as if she was an ambulance driver, Trudy sped through the hundred-mile trip to the clinic in a little over an hour.

Lydia ended up being admitted to the hospital for observation, even though Dr. Raymond, the eating disorder specialist, assured Trudy privately that he had seen girls far sicker. He went on to explain that Lydia was very dehydrated, and he was concerned enough about her heart to want to watch her closely for at least twelve hours.

Although Trudy refused to return home for the night, Dr. Raymond suggested she go get a cup of coffee or dinner while Lydia went through the lengthy admission process. She used the time to call Norm, unable to refrain from crying as she shared the news.

"Should I come to the hospital?" he asked, which made Trudy hesitate. She felt she had been given conflicting messages by Dr. Raymond, and wasn't sure what to think beyond worrying that Lydia would die.

After calling Dr. Raymond himself, Norm decided it was safe to check back in the next morning. Lydia ended up being discharged that day, but Dr. Raymond advised Trudy to have her attend the eating disorder program Mia had suggested. Trudy readily agreed, relieved to have someone taking action to help her daughter. Less enthusiastically, Lydia decided she would go, but only for a week.

The facility where Lydia was admitted by Dr. Raymond provided a number of different services, including his visits and an assessment by a psychiatrist specializing in eating disorders. There were also daily meetings with Randi, a nutritionist. Lydia seemed to like Randi, and spent hours reviewing the meal plans they developed.

The center offered educational and support groups for both Lydia and Trudy, and family therapy sessions that Norm and even Sean attended. In that session, Lydia revealed her sadness over Sean's departure for school, and her persistent feelings of being rejected by Norm. In turn, Norm talked about his perceptions that Lydia no longer wanted to visit him on weekends because of her busy social life.

Lydia was discharged from the eating disorder facility after two weeks, and continued to see Dr. Raymond once a month. In between, she checked in with Dr. Baker and Mary for weekly weigh-ins, and e-mailed Randi with her meal plans. Six months later, she had gained back most of her weight, and was noticeably happier. Her visits to Norm increased to twice a month, and she spent a weekend with Sean at his college during her spring break.

"I got so scared that day in Dr. Baker's office," she told Trudy one day, as they talked about what had happened. "When I heard her say I could die I knew I had to stop."

When a child is perceived to be near death, it's natural for moms and dads to want immediate intervention from physicians and therapists. Unfortunately, they often find themselves caught again in the "wait and see" maze mandated by insurance companies, unable to do much more than watch their children decline to a point dangerous enough to warrant more aggressive intervention.

As one parent pointed out to me, if a child was suspected of having cancer rather than anorexia, no one would take a "wait and see" approach, nor would the treatment process be so low key. Another said: "Even though she's twenty, if my daughter developed diabetes, someone would sit me down and explain everything. I would be taught how to prepare her meals, what the symptoms of low blood sugar were, the medication that might be used, and so on. With anorexia, I was told virtually nothing, supposedly because she was an adult, and this was a mental health problem."

Parents saw physicians as heroes, ready with medications that would make their children want to eat properly, special diets that would be the solution for months of either starvation or binging and purging, and therapy that would be like emotional surgery, cutting out the faulty area, reconnecting the healthy, and stitching up the whole situation. Of course, in all the interviews I conducted, this never happened.

In contrast, parents said their children referred to doctors as their enemies because they would encourage weight gain or at least an end to behaviors perceived to control weight. In addition to finding a medical doctor who was knowledgeable and able to relate well to both the parent and child, getting daughters and sons to the appointments was sometimes a challenge. "She literally refused to go. Wouldn't get in the car. Finally, an older neighbor she has a good relationship with slowly convinced her to get in the car and go for her appointment, but until then I was wondering what we were going to do. You can't force a teenager to go anywhere she doesn't want to go," said one father.

In the Beginning

When you arrive at the medical doctor's office, expect a lengthy battery of tests and questions as part of the initial assessment. (Again, *The Starving Family Workbook* has several pages to be completed ahead of time that may help streamline this process.)

Among other things, you and your child will be asked about weight changes, food behaviors like restricting, menstrual changes for girls, binging, and/or excess exercise. If a child purges, the doctor will want to know if he or she uses laxatives, diuretics ("water pills"), ipecac, or other substances to rid the body of food or fluid. There will be a careful "review of systems" to rule out other medical problems, and height and weight will be taken to calculate the Body Mass Index (BMI) which is the child's weight in kilograms divided by his or her height (in meters) squared. The physician will do a physical examination that evaluates every system of the body.

Sometimes, doctors ordered laboratory tests that gave parents an additional reassurance that their children were being well cared for. Some of the common diagnostic procedures a daughter or son with anorexia or bulimia may have required included:

Complete Blood Count (CBC): A sample of blood is taken, usually from the arm. When a child's weight is low, obtaining this sample could be painful and traumatic. One mom stood by, helpless, as several technicians attempted to draw blood from her extremely emaciated daughter's vein. "These patients are always challenges," the technician remarked, as the girl wept after each new needle stick. The test is valuable, because it can provide information on many medical conditions in addition to offering a "measuring stick" of nutrition and the components of the blood.

Electrocardiogram (ECG or EKG): This test is a harmless way to evaluate how well normal electrical impulses generated in the heart are being transmitted. To obtain an ECG, painless electrodes that can pick up the pattern of electrical impulses in the heart are attached with adhesive to the skin, and a tracing is made on graph paper. Sometimes this procedure is done in the physician's office, and at other times a special visit must be made to a cardiac clinic or department.

Chest X-Ray: This X-ray can offer further information on the size of the heart. X-rays of the spine and other bones can also be used to screen for damage. These X-rays resemble those taken to rule out broken bones after injury.

Bone Density Test: Performed by a doctor, this test uses sound waves to measure bone density. It does not hurt: a device called a sonometer is passed over the bones to obtain information on density, which can be impacted by malnutrition.

Urine Test: At the time of the visit, a sample of urine is often taken so simple tests can be performed in the doctor's office. These tests can indicate the balance of fluid in the body, and other parameters like glucose and protein. The results are one easy indicator of general kidney function.

Other Tests: A doctor may order other blood work to measure hormones, enzymes, proteins, electrolytes, vitamins, medication levels, and other substances. There are specific blood tests that can further evaluate the kidneys, liver, thyroid, and other important organs.

Paper and Pencil Tests: There are several screening tools that may be used by either a doctor or therapist to measure a child's attitudes about eating, self esteem, depression, and many other traits that are affected by eating disorders. Sometimes these tests may be mailed to you ahead of time for completion.

Focus on the Physical

Even after medical care was implemented for a child struggling with anorexia or bulimia parents continued to feel conflicted. They were relieved to have treatment underway, but they felt as if their role in caregiving was often negated by physicians, and that visits were rushed. A few even related the advice they were given was faulty:

"She [the pediatrician] told my daughter to eat foods she didn't eat even when she was well. You can imagine how that went over."

"Finding treatment is hard enough, but then when you do, most physicians aren't even fully informed of how to help."

"We waited up to an hour after traveling for an hour to see the doctor. Then it was ten minutes in and out, when I had a list of questions a mile long."

Caring at Its Best

Honesty about the physician's limitations was appreciated. One father talked about the first pediatrician his daughter visited, who admitted she was not prepared to deal with the special needs of a child with anorexia. The doctor did make sure the family had a referral to one of her colleagues with expertise, and the dad respected her for that.

When the doctor-patient relationship was positive, the support of a medical person was a great help. Doctors were viewed as the professionals who were protection against death: getting input on the physical aspects of health and knowing that the child's vital signs would be monitored regularly was reassuring.

Doctors were often the first people parents turned to when there were problems with medication, continued weight loss, or stomach problems. In situations like Lydia's, where life threatening complications like heart problems indicated a hospitalization was needed, the doctor was a much appreciated ally.

When a child's status became unstable, families found themselves more intensely involved with doctors and nurses, sometimes making long treks to visit several times a week.

Obviously, the level of parents' involvement with their children's physician varied with the son or daughter's age and life situation, but even when a child was technically an adult, there was still a need for some kind of communication or connection with medical providers during times of crisis.

It was helpful during these times of continuing contact to feel the relationship was personal as well as professional, and that the physician cared about the child and the family. Calls that were returned promptly, concerns that were addressed carefully, and little details like remembering a child's hobbies or interests all conveyed a sense of the doctor's investment in the relationship aspect of the treatment.

By monitoring the child's physical status, parents felt doctors helped share the emotional burden of care. Allowing him or her to assume part of that responsibility was of great benefit to parents.

"He said: 'Let me be the bad guy,'" one mom recalled. She was grateful that the physician took responsibility for weighing her daughter and setting up consequences for weight that got too low. In other cases, physicians collaborated with the treating therapist to identify acceptable weight parameters so both professionals could present a united front to the child and parent.

Challenges to Care

On the other side of medical care, families found the degree of misinformation among physicians upsetting. If generalists (pediatricians, family doctors, etc.) didn't understand eating disorders, specialists were even worse. Sometimes, parents even sensed a prejudice around anorexia or bulimia, as was the case with one mother whose daughter was referred to a gastroenterologist for reflux (a stomach problem that can occur with repeated vomiting):" He was almost ignorant, suggesting that my daughter was to blame for her problem, and giving the impression he wasn't eager to help. He did his job, but in contrast to our family doctor, he was clearly eager to get the visit over with."

It's not surprising that therapists and physicians can find it challenging and even frustrating to interact with parents who accord them superhuman powers to end a son or daughter's eating disorder. Few, if any, health care professionals will guarantee they can successfully reverse anorexia or bulimia, and it's probably best to be wary of those who do. Most will admit that anorexia and/or bulimia are mysterious illnesses no one completely understands. When there is no "cure" and that's a parent's most fervent desire, there are bound to be disappointments.

Nutritional Counseling

Dieticians, also part of the health care team, helped many families. In addition to giving the child information on the kinds and amounts of food he or she needed to eat, the nutritionist could help establish goals for gradual weight gain and maintenance. Another contribution was helping parents and children understand what foods were beneficial and that meals shouldn't be eaten alone. A few moms did note that their daughters often knew more about food than the nutritionists, and that their services, which often weren't covered by insurance, were expensive.

Finding Help

What do parents suggest looking for in a physician or therapist? My research revealed the following:

Look for:

- Someone with experience in eating disorders (a physician who is board certified in adolescent medicine is best)
- A person (professional training or specialization is irrelevant) who has worked with and understands the adolescent mindset
- A professional who recognizes the need to communicate with you — not about the intimate secrets your child shares with him or her, but about the overall status of your son or daughter
- Someone who isn't put off by your questions
- A person who treats you with respect
- Someone who isn't rushed — even if the visit is short, an attitude of calm and full attention can be given
- A person referred by someone who used that person for care of anorexia or bulimia
- A person who reinforces what you are doing <u>right</u>
- Someone who communicates honestly
- A person who shares the treatment plan
- Doctors who appreciate that you, too, are stressed

Avoid:

- A doctor or therapist whom you don't "connect" with from the very start
- Someone who tells you or your child to do things that don't feel right in your gut
- A person whose practice doesn't provide around the clock coverage — maybe you will never call during the off hours,

but there's a security in knowing someone will be available if you do. One mother was adamant: "Go by yourself and interview the person. Ask ahead of time if he or she is going to be willing to answer your questions, take emergency calls, etc."

The most important consideration mentioned in interviews was trust — on both the part of the parent and the child. Trust sometimes came from the physician or therapist making him or herself available to the entire family, and at other times it came from sharing information in a way that respected the child's privacy.

Again, parents suggested the best way to find an effective therapist or medical doctor was to ask for a recommendation from other parents who had gone through the same experience, but they also recognized that a person who worked well with one family might not suit others.

In rural areas, which are notably underserved, you may not have a choice of physicians, but parents in similar situations found creative ways to work with existing resources. One mother connected the family doctor with her son's treatment team of specialists, who were several hours away, but who willingly answered questions. Another parent provided selected research and clinical articles to a physician who hadn't worked with eating disorders.

If you are part of an insurance plan that mandates you to use certain pre-approved providers and feel your child is not getting the care needed, you still have options. One mother went out of her approved insurance network for initial care from a specialist, which she paid for herself. Once the child was stabilized, she returned to the approved provider and used the records she accumulated to document the necessity for the care her child received. After a bit of a battle, she received partial reimbursement. Another mother kept careful records of her daughter's vital signs and weight and used them as evidence for her HMO to approve out of network care. (You'll find more on these strategies in the chapter on insurance.)

LOCATING A DOCTOR
An Internet resource that can help locate a doctor is found at:

HTTP://DBAPPS.AMA-ASSN.ORG/APS/AMAHG.HTM
A searchable data base from the American Medical Association, does not list specialists in eating disorders but will provide a list of physicians within your zip code area with some basic information about each.

HTTP://WWW.PALE-REFLECTIONS.COM/
Pale Reflections is a valuable resource, oriented toward patients but with a treatment finder that simply can't be beat (access it through this homepage).

HTTP://SOMETHING-FISHY.ORG/TREATMENTFINDER.PHP AND HTTP://WWW.EDREFERRAL.COM ARE TWO OTHER WEBSITES FROM LARGE ORGANIZATIONS THAT OFFER INFORMATION PROVIDERS HAVE SENT THEM TO DESCRIBE THEIR SERVICES.

Superdoc

Clearly, it will be hard to find any one physician who meets all your expectations, but because he or she will be a vital part of your child's care, it's important to have a satisfying relationship with whomever you choose. Remember, too, that families can help or hinder the work of any health care professional in any situation where ongoing care is required.

When stress levels are high and you fear for your child's life, it's hard to be pleasant and patient with anyone. Living with this fear as a constant tension can interfere with how you interact with others, and sometimes, parents vent their frustration with illness at a health care provider. I've been an unhappy participant in the giving _and_ receiving end of that dynamic, so I understand how both parties feel!

A positive relationship between provider and "patient" will benefit everyone. Look over the list of suggested guidelines from parents on the preceding pages. Ask how you would rate the relevant items if a doctor was choosing _you_ as a patient. Recognize that you both have expectations of each other, and don't hesitate to periodically check in to see whether those expectations are being met.

RESOURCES

If you would like more detailed descriptions of the medical tests and procedures described within this chapter, check these websites, or search for articles on "medical tests for eating disorders."

http://www.cnn.com/HEALTH/library/DS/00294.html
MayoClinic.com.

http://www.nationaleatingdisorders.org/
p.asp?WebPage_ID=324&Profile_ID=68736
National Eating Disorder's page on "Suggested Medical Tests."

http://www.denverhealth.org/ACUTE/document/diagnosis_AN.pdf
Denver Health website on medical treatment of eating disorders.

http://aappolicy.aappublications.org/cgi/content/full/pediatrics;111/1/204#T3
Article on diagnosis of anorexia or bulimia in adolescents for pediatricians.

8
Talk About It

༄༅

"I CALL THERAPY THE 'SHAME AND BLAME' GAME." A PARENT

"IF PARENTS AREN'T PATHOLOGICAL WHEN THIS PROCESS STARTS, THEY WILL BE BY THE END." A THERAPIST

When Rebecca, a perky sixteen year old, confessed to her parents that she had been bulimic for two years, they immediately searched for a therapist to address this serious problem. Although Rebecca had kept her eating disorder a secret to that point, her mother Ann and father Dan immediately responded to her revelation with an action plan to help.

Dan describes their first therapist as a person who clearly had "issues" around food and girls with eating disorders: "Her approach was to try and scold Rebecca so she wouldn't binge and purge. We went to her for six months. Sometimes she had family sessions, which she tried to get us all to attend. My son Rob went along once and walked out. He told us later we should ditch her — he was right."

The next therapist Ann found was a social worker who said she specialized in eating disorders. Both parents sighed in relief, believing they had finally found someone who would nudge Rebecca along the road to recovery. This therapist turned out to be a bigger disaster than the first, since she instructed

Rebecca not to listen to her parents, and wouldn't give Ann and Dan any information about their daughter.

"I think you should back off," she told Ann after one session with Rebecca. "The last thing your daughter needs right now is parents who are overly controlling."

Although Rebecca had maintained her weight to that point, while seeing the second therapist the pounds began to drop and her behaviors switched to anorexic. Alarmed, Ann contacted the therapist and requested a family session, but was told this was impossible for reasons of confidentiality.

When Rebecca took an overdose of Tylenol and ended up in the hospital, Ann and Dan decided they were finished with the second therapist. They made dozens of calls to get suggestions on someone who could help their daughter, and ended up locating Inez, a therapist whose office was at a university health center one hour from their rural Texas home.

For six months, Ann drove Rebecca to and from her therapy sessions. Both she and Dan noticed their daughter was improving, and, on her seventeenth birthday they bought her a used car and gave her permission to drive herself to see Inez. Rebecca continued the visits for another six months, making steady progress until both she and the therapist decided weekly sessions were no longer necessary. Gradually, the appointments tapered until Rebecca was a student in the same college where Inez worked. She dropped in to see Inez as needed, usually at least once a month. The relationship between Rebecca and her third therapist was so beneficial that Ann describes it as "the turning point."

"Inez understands Rebecca, and she works with us, too. When Rebecca started to backslide during her freshman year in college Inez called us and let us know they were increasing the frequency of their visits, but that she thought everything would be okay. I appreciated that so much, and although we worried, we also recognized that Rebecca had a big plus going for her with Inez."

Therapy, and all its implications, can be a threatening if not paralyzing prospect for many families. In the hours of conversations with parents, I heard a lot about therapists, most of it negative. I offer the following disclaimer: Can any mom or dad who is already stressed by caregiving feel positive about sharing a very negative experience with a complete stranger? Is there any way to expose your every joy and sorrow to an outsider without feeling vulnerable? Many described having a therapist become almost like an extra but unwelcome family member — this was true for me, too.

Catch-22

The very nature of a therapeutic relationship is complicated. On one hand, in lieu of a doctor "curing" an eating disorder, therapists were seen as the next best bet. However, turning to someone else with this expectation can feel like an open admission of failure, and the act of scheduling an appointment to share the intimate details of family life can seem like a very public surrender. While medical care rarely reflects on the quality of mothering or fathering (no one seems to connect urinalysis results with parenting skills), therapy has the potential to do just that.

Even if a family isn't proactive like Ann and Dan, they will eventually end up working with a therapist. Stabilization of the child's medical status and weight is always a priority, but then some type of mental health therapy will usually be advocated. Sometimes the number of tries it took to find a good fit between therapist and child was simply astounding: one father counted six different individuals his child saw for varying lengths of time before finding a person they all worked well with.

Several parents suggested "interviewing" prospective therapists to get a feel for their style. Another thought it was valuable to observe the child's interactions with the therapist to get a sense of the dynamic between them. She said to pay particularly close attention to the first contact, as it's often an important indicator of how the relationship will develop.

In this chapter's story, Ann felt an instant connection with Inez when the therapist took her aside, gave her a business card, and said either Dan or she should call immediately if they noticed any changes in Rebecca. This simple gesture recognized that she was the full-time caregiver and expert on Rebecca. Ann also remembered that Inez didn't mind being questioned about her treatment philosophy, and that she adopted an attitude of "mutual transparency," sharing her goals for Rebecca with Dan and Ann on a regular basis.

When a parent or parents arrived at the door of the therapist with their child, they often had the same expectations for a quick fix they took to the medical doctor's office, as reflected by the following comments:

"I just kept asking her [therapist] to tell me what to do to make my daughter better, but she kept evading me."

"Therapy was the most frustrating part of this whole experience. No one had any answers for us."

"So I thought, let's just get her into therapy, and this will all get taken care of."

Like the parents who made these remarks, many others were frustrated rather than satisfied with the psychiatric care they were offered. They already felt as if they had failed their eating disordered child, so admitting a stranger into the intimate circle of their lives was threatening at best and terrifying at worst. Ann and Dan, like many parents, said they approached each new therapeutic relationship with a sense of both despair and hope.

The Hunt for Help

The more practical and pragmatic side of finding a therapist who would work with an eating disordered child was often challenging. Some counselors simply refused to treat children with anorexia or bulimia, while others did so on a limited basis (i.e., they were part-time and only available for certain hours).

One mom said: "I mean I sat here with a list of twenty numbers and cried through all of them as they shut me off one after the other and I just kept saying, 'Well, do you have someone else I can call?'"

Sometimes even highly recommended therapists were a poor fit for a particular family. In one case, after six months, the therapist took the child's parents aside and said she didn't think the relationship was working, and that she wasn't the best person to care for their daughter. The relationship ended on a positive note because of her honesty, and her follow up referral to a colleague who readily agreed to see the patient was appreciated.

Families drove incredible distances to obtain help: one mother, father, and college-age sibling dedicated three hours a week (one way) to transporting a young woman to a clinic for treatment. At other times, even locating a therapist was impossible in rural areas.

However, even the best therapist could not motivate a child who wasn't ready to recover. A father summarized it this way: "When your daughter has an eating disorder you are desperate and you want immediate results. Therapy doesn't provide that. It helps express feelings, but until your child sees a need to change, they won't."

"Don't expect anything for the first four months," another suggested.

Sometimes, the gender of the therapist was the same as the child being treated, but not always. While professional background and personal characteristics didn't seem to matter, experience with eating disorders did.

"Even if they think they can help but have no experience, don't use them!" advised one parent who had trusted a novice. Another mother went further and suggested that only therapists trained in the last ten years should be considered, adding: "Ask them specifically how many cases they have treated, and what the outcomes were."

Parents suggested finding a therapist who has a "track record" of work with adolescents and someone whom you would feel comfortable seeing individually (even if this will never happen). Counselors who badgered children or were paternalistic often alienated both the child and parent.

The Obstacles

There were many troubling experiences reported by parents. Some therapists gave blatantly wrong information that skewed the course of therapy. One told a young teen not to listen to what her parents suggested because they were "too controlling." In another instance, a family was advised to avoid residential care at all costs when this turned out to be the very intervention (which they sought on their own) that they felt helped their daughter recover.

One therapist told a mother not to be so involved with her daughter; another was less tactful, telling the mom to "butt out." In contrast, another counselor suggested a mom become more involved with her daughter, and make her the primary focus of their family life.

A father noticed that the therapist focused exclusively on his wife, blaming her for the child's eating disorder. Another father commented that he, too, was completely ignored while his wife was bombarded with suggestions for change.

Desperate to do what would be helpful for their children, many parents reported following a therapist's advice, even when it was counterintuitive.

"What was I thinking?" one mother asked, remembering how she allowed her severely underweight daughter to dictate what she would and wouldn't eat because a therapist advised her to do so. (Her daughter ended up in a medical crisis a short time later.)

"Why did I go against my own instinct?" another pondered, recalling an incident where she took a therapist's advice and didn't discipline her daughter for breaking family rules. She felt this created an ongoing pattern of "making exceptions" for her child because of the severity of her bulimia.

Another frustration was inconsistency. Parents whose children went through multiple therapists found that one set of suggested interventions often contradicted what they had been told previously. Some examples:

- Allowing or not allowing use of diet foods
- Encouraging the child to vent emotions (especially anger) in any way she or he saw fit, which included screaming, punching pillows, cursing, throwing things, etc. versus stressing that the child should express emotions in a way that was respectful of others
- Wanting parents to provide limits and control for the child as compared to having parents adopt a "hands-off" approach
- Using weight as an incentive, not using weight as an incentive
- Allowing child to prepare food, not allowing child to prepare food
- Weighing frequently versus not weighing at all
- Establishing negative consequences for weight loss versus not attaching judgment to weight loss

Rather than criticize the correctness of any specific approach, parents were baffled by the lack of consensus on what their role should or should not be with an eating disordered child. What one therapist approved, earned a "dysfunctional" label from another.

Wounding with Words

Children came to therapy willingly at times and under duress at others. Anger and denial was common and sometimes this negative mindset influenced what the son or daughter told a counselor about family situations. It was distressing when therapists based their approach on what the child shared with them, because sometimes the information was biased or even untrue, as happened to this mom:

"My son's therapist called me in for a session and I was blown away by what happened. She confronted me about my 'emotional isolation' and failure to support my son's attempts to recover. I asked if she knew that I had used all my vacation days from work to drive him to an eating disorder clinic the year before, or if she knew that I had convinced my husband to use most of our savings account to pay for the parts of his treatment that insurance wouldn't cover. I went on to tell her about an average day in our house, and how much of my time went to trying to help my son. She was dumbfounded by the end of it...maybe I confirmed her worst beliefs about me with the tirade, but I really felt blindsided. I told my son I didn't know what more I could do for him. It hurt, it really did."

Other parents had similar stories of "betrayal" by their children, and therapists who confronted them about incidents taken out of context or misrepresented by their sons or daughters. Therefore, another criteria for a therapist is to find someone who listens to all sides of the story.

"Listening to all sides of the story" took on another perspective relating to a child's progress toward recovery or lack thereof. One father described how adept his daughter became at gaining just enough weight and voicing just the right intentions to get discharged from treatment and begin her eating disordered lifestyle all over again. He and many other parents felt it was critical to find care providers who would see through and curtail a child's attempts to manipulate.

Relationship Rapport

When a therapist who worked well with them was located, parents expressed great relief and appreciation for the help such a person could provide:

"My child's connection with her therapist was what helped her."

"Whatever you have to do to find a good therapist, do it. They're the single most important thing to help your child."

Once a relationship was established, there were differing opinions on how involved a parent should be with their child's therapist. One mom found herself actually seeing her child's therapist for counseling, and said that despite the challenge to maintain confidentiality, the arrangement proved very beneficial.

"If I can see results, I don't need her therapist to give me updates," said one parent who was satisfied with allowing her child and the therapist to relate without input from her. Many others were uncomfortable or even angry with being treated like an "outsider" and being denied any feedback from the therapist.

"When I'm paying the deductible for therapy, which is a healthy chunk of change from my own pocket, I have a right to know how things are going. I certainly wouldn't pay a consultant to do work for me which is kept a big secret," one parent argued.

Dan felt that same way. He pointed out that since he was the source of payment for the therapy Rebecca received, he should be entitled to updates and information. For this reason, he was satisfied when Inez called to notify them about the freshman backslide, and trusted that she would do so if future problems occurred. This, he noted, was a direct contrast from the way Rebecca's first two therapists operated. It was reassuring when Inez told Dan and Ann that her policy was to obtain blanket permission to talk with parents at her first session with a new patient.

When the relationship with therapists was extended, parents said they wanted these things:

- Concrete suggestions on how to help their children
- A focus on the children rather than on the parents
- Having a plan for action and follow up in case of emergencies
- Holding children accountable for their own behavior
- Measurable results, even if they were small
- Offering explanations of behavior and information
- Help with the guilt parents felt
- An understanding of what parents of a child with eating disorders go through
- Avoid judging or labeling

The perception that physicians and therapists were accepting and nonjudgmental was very important to families. Ann recalls that while Rebecca's first two therapists conveyed an attitude of disapproval, Inez had faith in the family's ability to recover. She was one who set the relationship on a positive course, as happened with another mom:

"She [the therapist] let us know from the start that she didn't believe families 'caused' eating disorders."

Food for the Family

Sometimes, a therapist would want to work with the entire family. There were two ways in which this seemed to happen:

either the child's treating therapist would have occasional sessions with all members of the family, or the parents would seek out a separate therapist who worked exclusively with everyone.

One dad noted that: "We had numerous short term family therapists during every hospitalization, and each one recreated the wheel. In the end, a family therapist we found on our own helped much more. With the others it was going through the motions: okay, who should we focus on and blame for her eating disorder today? Sometimes it was my wife, sometimes me, and once it was even my son."

Many inpatient facilities where children received treatment for eating disorders required a "Family Week" where parents, siblings, and any other relatives intimately involved in the child's life were asked to attend. During that week they participated in an intensive program that often combined therapy and education. These experiences were uniformly reported positively for a number of reasons.

First, "Family Week" provided an opportunity to compare an individual child to others, and "normalize" his or her behavior a bit. Second, the week often offered expert input from a variety of specialists. Even parents of children with long-term illnesses gleaned new ideas and information. Third, these kinds of Family Weeks recognized the involvement of siblings. Not only would brothers and sisters get the opportunity to meet other siblings who were living with a child who had an eating disorder, they would also have the chance to express their own feelings about the illness of their brother or sister. In turn, the children with eating disorders could also talk honestly with their siblings. Finally, Family Week gave parents a venue to dialogue with other parents who were going through similar experiences.

The Company of Others

In addition to family programs connected with inpatient treatment, some parents attended support groups in their community. Some groups were led by a therapist, while others were parent-led. The reports were mixed, and seemed to vary according to the facilitator (professional versus parent) and format (structured versus unstructured). Two parents said:

"I went because I felt obligated to go after her doctor suggested it. But I didn't really find it of much benefit — it was often a complaint session." (This parent attended a professionally led group that she felt was not adequately guided by the leader.)

"You learn a lot at a support group — like what other girls are doing. The behaviors are incredible. And I got some good ideas on how to deal with the insurance company." (This caregiver participated in a group led by other parents.)

Him, Her, Us, and Me

Many parents found that when their daughter or son became ill, for the first time they would begin seeing a therapist themselves, either individually or as a couple. Says one dad:

"Therapy wasn't helping my child, so my wife and I went instead."

"At a minimum, parents should go to therapy because they need help talking about what they are feeling and experiencing," a mother suggested.

"Find a good therapist for you as well as her — you'll need it," one parent advised.

Another parent commented on the "multitude" of therapists involved with his family: both mother and father had individual therapists, as did their daughter. The entire family saw a therapist together, and their "healthy" son had just been scheduled for an appointment with yet another counselor.

Connect to Disconnect

In my travels and talks, I've spoken with many professionals and parents about eating disorders. Often, the therapeutic relationship has been a "hot topic," leading me to ask both groups about what an ideal interaction should be like. Not surprisingly, the answers don't match well (see the list of comments in Appendix A).

Is it possible to create positive connections between parents and professionals who are both providing different kinds of emotional care for a child with anorexia or bulimia? As an informed and empowered mom or dad, make a plan to accomplish this between yourself and the therapists you know. It will make a difference for both you and the child you love.

SOME COMMON TYPES OF
THERAPIES USED WITH EATING DISORDERS

These are very simple and general descriptions of terms you may hear used in relation to therapy.

Cognitive Behavioral Therapy (CBT) is a time limited form of "talk therapy" that focuses on the relationship between thoughts and behaviors. It's one of the more popular approaches used with eating disorders.

Interpersonal Psychotherapy looks at sources of stress, particularly in relation to food, and explores interpersonal patterns of relating.

Psychodynamic Psychotherapy is a nondirective therapy that works on getting the patient to gain insight into his or her motivations. It may focus on the recognition and expression of repressed conflicts.

Self Help and Guided Self Help involve minimal therapeutic contact and instead encourage patients to support each other in a safe environment.

Dialectic Behavioral Therapy (DBT) is like CBT but more directive. It combines behavior therapy and Eastern philosophy for an approach that suggests first acceptance of oneself and then change.

Eye Movement Desensitization and Reprocessing (EMDR) is a unique form of psychotherapy that uses eye movements or rhythmical stimulation to "repattern" the brain's processing system. It's thought to work especially well for people who have experienced trauma.

Psychoeducational Approach stresses an understanding of the why, what, and how of eating disorders, then looks at how change might occur.

Addictions Model views eating disorders as an addictive process, much like substance addiction, and uses the Twelve Step Model as structure.

Family Therapy could either involve helping a child explore family dynamics on his or her own, or involving several or all family members in sessions of therapy. The belief underlying this approach is that the family unit functions as a system, and that a child's eating disorder is part of the bigger family dynamic.

Expressive Therapies such as art and movement can be alternative ways to explore the body and feelings.

Eclectic Approach can be any combination of therapies.

Note: Many therapists will tailor their therapeutic approach to whether the child has anorexia or bulimia

RESOURCES

There are several online support groups that might be helpful if you lack access to an in-person group:

http://health.groups.yahoo.com/group/milestonesinrecovery/
This is a free online support group from a treatment center.

http://www.joannapoppink.com/supportgroups/supportgroups.html
One woman's discussion forum about eating disorders.

http://www.healthyplace.com/Communities/Eating_Disorders/Site/comm_calender.htm
This site offers several online discussions and chats specific to various aspects of eating disorders.

http://www.something-fishy.org/online/options.php
This site is part of a larger organization for eating disorders.

If you would like an in-person group, check the following:

http://home.comcast.net/~rpike20625/freed/
This is a family supported organization that helps others locate support groups and resources in their communities. Can also be contacted through:
FREED
9611 Page Avenue (Web)
Bethesda, MD 20814-1737
Telephone: (301) 585-0358 or (301) 493-4568
E-mail: You may send e-mail to bigmommary@aol.com.

http://www.anad.org/site/anadweb/section.php?id=6602
The National Association of Anorexia Nervosa and Related Disorders offers both online resources and a searchable data base to find an eating disorder support group in your area.

9
Pills for Their Ills: Using Medications for Eating Issues

అఆ

"WHEN HER DOCTOR SUGGESTED AN ANTIDEPRESSANT I SAID OKAY, AND I'LL TAKE ONE TOO." *A MOTHER OF A TEEN GIRL WITH ANOREXIA*

Carol received a call from her daughter Lisa's college infirmary at the end of February. The nurse on the other end explained she had been given permission to telephone and talk with Carol. The doctor at the infirmary felt Lisa needed to start antidepressant medication to treat her bulimia, but wanted to let her parents know about it.

Confused, Carol asked why antidepressant medication would be used, remembering the many articles she'd read about the side effects of such drugs. Further, she told the nurse she didn't think Lisa was depressed, but that her long struggle with bulimia was the explanation for any problems with her mood. Once the eating disorder got better, everything else would improve.

When Lisa's dad Ed came home that night, Carol questioned whether she'd done the right thing. Ed didn't hesitate to agree that she had — he'd also seen a recent television show that suggested antidepressants actually increased the risk of suicide.

A short time later the front door opened and Lisa burst into the house. She'd driven two hours from her school to see her parents, and was clearly upset.

Carol and Ed hadn't seen their daughter since winter break a month earlier, and they were shocked by the change in her appearance. Her eyes had deep circles underneath them, and the long brown hair that was always a source of pride was now dull and unkempt. Although Lisa's weight seemed to still be within normal range or even slightly over, she was wearing a baggy sweatshirt and sweatpants that hadn't been washed in awhile.

"I can't take it anymore!" Lisa cried, collapsing into her mother's arms. She went on to tell her parents that she was failing all her classes and fighting daily with the roommate she'd gotten along with during fall semester.

"She hates me! She's spread rumors all over the dorm about me vomiting in our bathroom."

Lisa, Carol, and Ed talked about what to do for a long time, without reaching a conclusion. Ed went to bed, but Carol found herself sitting by Lisa's bed for a long time, rubbing her daughter's back and reflecting on the call she had received that morning. As soon as it was reasonable to expect their family doctor to be in her office, she called and explained the situation to the office nurse, who scheduled an appointment for Lisa that afternoon.

Dr. Pace had seen Lisa twice over Christmas break, knowing that her bulimia was still active but stable. Although Lisa's weight had been normal, at the second visit she had admitted to sleep problems and occasional irritability. She associated those with normal college adjustment, and assured the doctor she was doing well overall.

Something about the visit bothered Dr. Pace enough to call the doctor at the infirmary (with Lisa's permission) and tell him she thought Lisa should be seen as soon as she returned to school. Now, seeing the obvious change in Lisa's status, she excused herself and called the college again to discuss the recommendation for medication that had been made.

"My suggestion is that we try the antidepressant," she informed Carol and Lisa when she returned to the exam room. "It seems that Lisa is really struggling to deal with her eating disorder, but it's hard to get by day-to-day. Would you agree with that?" she asked.

"Yes," Lisa answered, her face covered by her hands.

"But I thought those drugs were dangerous. I've read about the side effects, and it really makes me nervous," Carol protested. "Lisa told me last night she didn't want to take them either."

Dr. Pace listened to Carol and Lisa's concerns about medication. She then explained that antidepressants were often used to help combat the depressed mood that typically accompanies an eating disorder. These depressive moods can make it more difficult for a patient to respond to other medical and psychological treatments.

"Lisa says she has no energy and isn't sleeping. If we can help her with those problems, she might be able to work on the eating disorder, too. And some girls have found that the antidepressant that the doctor from the college suggested works to take the edge off the compulsion to binge and purge." Dr.

Pace waited for Carol or Lisa to respond, then took out a sample package of the antidepressant medication and literature on how it worked. "How about trying it for a month, and then if there's no difference after that, we'll regroup?"

As Carol and Lisa drove home, they discussed what to do next. After reading over the information Dr. Pace had given her, Lisa sighed and said she had become desperate, and wanted to drop out of school for the semester and live at home. Carol agreed this might be best, and even thought to herself that it might be time to try medication.

For two weeks after starting the antidepressant, Lisa was inconsolable, crying every day and unable to control her vomiting. Carol and Ed could barely stand to leave for work in the morning, wondering what state their daughter would be in during the day. They were comforted by Dr. Pace's ability to connect Lisa with a new therapist who had suffered and recovered from bulimia.

Little by little, Lisa began to show signs of an improved mood. Carol noticed that her daughter began to shower each day and wash her hair, and Ed was pleased when Lisa agreed to come to the restaurant he managed and help him with some paperwork for a day. One month after starting on medication, Lisa applied for a job in a daycare center, and told her parents she was feeling much better. Although her bulimia was still a serious problem, her mood had improved enough for her to feel she could hold down a job while working with the therapist to address the eating disorder.

Over the next three months, Lisa improved more than she had in the last three years. She stayed on the medication, without experiencing any side effects. The following fall she returned to school and picked up her studies again.

This chapter is meant to share experiences of other families, and should not be considered a definitive resource on drugs, doses, or diagnoses, or a medical recommendation specific to your child. The focus is on the types of medications parents reported being used to treat their sons' and daughters' eating disorders, their thoughts about using such drugs, and whether they seemed to be beneficial.

Parents had a multitude of opinions about the use of medications. They also reported a range of outcomes when pharmaceuticals were used. Sometimes, they really were a "fix" of sorts, leading to dramatic improvements in a child's ability to recover from his or her eating disorder. One parent I spoke with emailed me months after our conversation to let me know her son was doing "incredibly well" after starting a new medication. It's possible that in some cases, adding medication to counseling made a dramatic difference and that neither therapy would have been as effective alone.

For others, there was either no noticeable effect or even a worsening of the child's condition. Although some parents might not have noticed an effect, it's entirely possible that medication did work to keep a child stable or prevent an even worse decline in health.

Says this father: "She has been on an extraordinary amount: every antidepressant and antipsychotic as well as medication for her stomach and digestion. They have kept her alive but not made her any better."

In almost every case, it was suggested at some point in the course of the eating disorder that a psychotropic medication could be of benefit. The term "psychotropic" is a catchall description for antidepressants, anti-anxiety agents, and a host of other drugs designed to address some aspect of mental health. Increasingly, they are thought to be of benefit for young women and men who have anorexia or bulimia.

The major kinds of psychotropic medications that parents described being used for their children (and which are representative of those used elsewhere) include:

Antidepressants: For children like Lisa who had a noticeable depression along with their eating disorder, antidepressant medications were often prescribed as an adjunct to psychotherapy with a counselor.

Anti-anxiety: If a child had a high anxiety level, which was seen to be driving the eating disorder, these medications were used on a short-term basis.

Mood stabilizers: In a few cases where there were questions about a child having bipolar disorder, medications were used to try and help stabilize mood so extreme ups and downs wouldn't exacerbate anorexia or bulimia.

Anti-psychotics: When a child's thoughts were particularly disordered, these medications were used to clear thinking. The parents whose children received anti-psychotics reported a beneficial effect, but these were only a few of the many I interviewed.

Sticker Shock

For some parents, the suggestion of using medications came as a relief because it was a tangible therapy that they hoped would "cure" their children in the same way as antibiotics are used to clear up infections.

"This I understood," one father shared. "A pill. When you're sick, you take a pill and you get better. I was happy to hear it."

This same man was shocked when he stopped after work to pick up the medication and discovered the price tag that came with it: "Then I thought, it doesn't matter how much it costs, this is her life we're talking about."

Others were more like Carol, with either the parent and/ or the daughter needing more convincing before being ready to try medication.

"After much arguing, she agreed to try an antidepressant. Her moods are great, eating habits relatively normal, and she's not upset about gaining twenty pounds," says one mom, whose daughter was ambivalent about medications.

Another mother described how her child ended up on medication: "It was a difficult decision. My daughter didn't want 'pills' because she had heard so many negative things." As with Lisa, this girl's therapist suggested trying it for one month. "The therapist said she would discontinue it if it didn't feel right. She explained it to my daughter this way: you need help right now, and this is something that's hard to do on your own. That helped a lot because then my daughter didn't see it as a failure." (And she added later that the antidepressant that was prescribed did indeed seem to help.)

If medications were changed, weren't in the approved formulary, or if the insurance company felt there were loopholes that allowed denial of coverage, parents sometimes had to pay out of pocket for prescriptions. Even though they would eventually recover part or all of the hundreds of dollars of their own money they spent on drugs, it was often a bitter and long process to do so. One family spent $1200 to $1300 of its own money every month on medication. Sometimes, physicians can offer free samples of medications, or drug companies have special "patient assistance programs" that help offset these expenses.

PRESCRIPTION DRUG
PATIENT ASSISTANCE PROGRAMS

SEVERAL PRESCRIPTION DRUG PATIENT ASSISTANCE PROGRAMS ARE AVAILABLE AT THESE WEBSITES. MANY HAVE ELIGIBILITY REQUIREMENTS BASED ON INCOME AND A DOCTOR'S CONSENT:

HTTP://WWW.NAMI.ORG/CONTENT/CONTENTGROUPS/HELPLINE1/PRESCRIPTION_DRUG_PATIENT_ASSISTANCE
THIS EXCELLENT RESOURCE FROM THE NATIONAL ALLIANCE FOR THE MENTALLY ILL PROVIDES A CHART OF WHICH DRUGS ARE COVERED BY SPECIFIC PHARMACEUTICAL COMPANIES, AND HOW TO CONTACT THEM FOR FURTHER INFORMATION.

HTTP://WWW.NEEDYMEDS.COM/INDICES/ARTICLE.SHTML
THE NEEDY MEDS PROGRAM ITSELF OFFERS SOME EXPENSIVE RESOURCES THAT YOUR PHYSICIAN OR THERAPIST MAY WANT TO PURCHASE, BUT AT THIS LOCATION ON ITS SITE DR. RICHARD SAGALL OFFERS AN INFORMATIVE SUMMARY ON PATIENT ASSISTANCE PROGRAMS.

HTTP://WWW.HELPINGPATIENTS.ORG/INDEX.CFM
THIS SITE IS RUN BY PHRMA AND ITS 48 MEMBER COMPANIES, WHICH CLAIM TO HAVE OFFERED FREE PRESCRIPTION MEDICINES TO 6.2 MILLION PATIENTS IN THE U.S. IN 2003. THE SEARCHABLE DATA BASE ALLOWS YOU TO ENTER THE MEDICINE YOU ARE SEARCHING FOR, PROGRAMS OFFERED BY SPECIFIC COMPANIES, AND EMAIL UPDATES.

Eventual Effect

Although Lisa responded well enough to the antidepressant (and perhaps her new therapist) to return to school, she wasn't completely free of her bulimia. Today, her parents know she purges during times of stress, but they believe overall her health is much better, largely because of the antidepressant she continues to take.

It was different for Jan, another young adult woman whose anorexia began in college and lasted for many years after. At one point, Jan was so ill her physician urged her parents to seek inpatient treatment in a hospital or eating disorder center. They did this, and although they were grateful for the treatment Jan received there, her mother wondered if the use of medications was excessive.

"The approach was to give the girls medication, a lot of medication, so they were so drugged up it didn't matter to them that they were eating and gaining weight. Jan was on so many medications I didn't even know what they all were, but they helped her stabilize and she even began to put on a few pounds."

When Jan was discharged and came home to live with her parents, she told her mother she was having problems thinking straight, and was engaging in some self-injuring behavior. At that point, Jan decided to stop all of the medications she had been started on in the treatment facility. She talked to her regular doctor and he helped develop a schedule to wean her off the drugs. After a month, her mother said Jan felt much better and all the "strange ideas" (of self harm) went away.

Sometimes, the child's health was so compromised parents were told certain antidepressants couldn't be used: "The doctor told us these medications wouldn't work right away because she needed to improve her nutritional status first. Once she was in therapy and eating they put her on an antidepressant so she was getting three things at once. We don't know which one of those things worked, but we don't care. She got better."

A Bit of Better

Sometimes, medications affected behaviors that were connected with the anorexia or bulimia but not the eating disorder itself. For Jan, this was depression. In another case, a child's volatile mood swings lessened when she began taking a mood stabilizing medication also used to treat seizures. Another mother noticed a "phenomenal change from one day to the next" when her daughter went on medication: "To be honest, I had such a hard time putting her on that medication just because of all the stigma and everything else to deal with. I thought: 'Oh no, not my daughter,' and now that is the least of my worries. If she's on it the rest of her life that doesn't bother me if it keeps her on an even keel so she can do the stuff she needs to do."

Many of the behaviors connected with eating disorders were attributed to malnutrition, which no medication can treat. Without sufficient calories and nutrients, the best drugs in the world cannot reverse an eating disorder, one mother believed. She said: "When your child isn't eating, her brain isn't functioning properly. When her brain doesn't function, she won't eat properly. It's a cycle. That's why good nutrition is the best medicine. Food for an anorexic is like chemotherapy to a cancer patient."

All of this is important to know in making decisions about medication. Each type of drug will impact each child differently, and side effects will occur for some and not others. Just as with other forms of treatment, there is no pill that will "cure" eating disorders — if there was, someone would be very rich right now.

RESOURCES
There are resources on medications at the websites below:

http://www.mental-health-matters.com/articles/article.php?artID=236
This website is offered from the National Institute for Mental Health, and offers a medications booklet that details what medications are used for mental health disorders in general, their side effects, and other information.

http://www.somersetmedicalcenter.com/15084.cfm
This is a nice page from Somerset Medical Center with specific information about medications used for eating disorders.

http://www.edreferral.com/medications_for_ed.htm
This page is prepared by the International Association for Eating Disorders and refers specifically to medications for eating disorders.

http://www.something-fishy.org/doctors/medications.php
Provides: "Basic information about some of the most common medications prescribed in helping to treat *some* sufferers of Eating Disorders."

10
Partial, Total, In and Out: Programs and Hospital Stays for Treatment of Eating Disorders

౭৽৵৻

"OUR THERAPIST TOLD US RESIDENTIAL CARE WAS THE WORST THING THAT COULD HAPPEN, SO OF COURSE WE DIDN'T EVEN CONSIDER IT. BUT FINALLY IT CAME TO THAT POINT, AND TO BE HONEST, I THINK IT SAVED OUR DAUGHTER'S LIFE." *FATHER OF A GIRL WITH ANOREXIA/BULIMIA*

"DOES IT STRIKE YOU AS ODD TO TAKE A BUNCH OF GIRLS WITH A FIXATION ON FOOD AND PUT THEM ALL TOGETHER FOR DAYS AND EVEN WEEKS IN A SETTING WHERE THE GOAL IS TO GAIN WEIGHT?" *A PHYSICIAN WHO TREATS EATING DISORDERS*

Franny Thompson's eating disorder was clearly getting worse. At seventeen, she'd been in her community hospital several times for cutting and malnutrition, discharged each time after a stay of five days or less because she gained enough weight to meet the minimum requirements.

After her fifth hospitalization, she told her mother Beth that she couldn't see the purpose of living with the constant cycle of binge, purge, and then restrict, which had escalated out of her control. Her cutting was also becoming more of a problem; on a regular basis she inflicted some type of self harm.

Her parents Ruth and Matt became even more anxious about her wellbeing, and asked her pediatrician what he would suggest. Dr. Wells had diagnosed her with anorexia eighteen months earlier, and had referred the Thompsons to Nick, a local therapist specialized in eating disorders. Dr. Wells also recommended a nutritionist whom the Thompsons paid out-of- pocket for weekly counseling visits with Franny. In short, he told them, he had done all that he could within the limits of his abilities. Nick agreed that Franny needed a different approach than they'd been using, and offered to call a colleague who was an expert in eating disorders.

A few days later, Nick provided the Thompsons with the names of several facilities that offered specialized treatment of eating disorders. He explained that in contrast to their community hospital, Franny would stay at the facility for a longer time, and could even participate in an aftercare program that would help her transition back into life at home.

From her research on the Internet, Ruth recognized several of the names. She began making calls, and within a week Franny had been assessed by telephone and was judged appropriate for admission to Brookton (pseudonym). Another week passed before a bed was available, which meant Franny had to go back to Dr. Wells and be reassessed in order for Matt's insurance to approve the admission.

Ruth, Matt, and Franny's younger brother Cliff all made the four hour trip to Brookton. Ruth recalls stifling her tears as they drove, and feeling terrified inside. She hated seeing her daughter so far away, but she also hated the disease that was consuming Franny's life. In the back seat, Franny and Cliff were subdued. Instead of bickering as they might at other times when forced to ride together, they each listened to music on their CD players, lost in their own worlds.

At Brookton, an admissions counselor met the Thompsons and took Franny's belongings, which would be searched for sharp objects or other contraband like medication or food. She reviewed Brookton's visiting policy, which was limited to weekends only.

"But frankly, Mrs. Thompson, from what we hear of your relationship with Franny, it might be best if you two didn't see each other for awhile," the admissions counselor commented.

Ruth felt as if she'd been punched in the stomach. Nick had never mentioned any issues that concerned him about the family. When she looked at Franny questioningly, her daughter turned her head away defiantly.

During the first week of her admission, Franny refused to eat all of her meals, and lost two pounds. This led to a restriction of her phone calls, so Ruth and Matt weren't even allowed to talk to her for five long days. Ruth agonized over what might be happening to her daughter during that time, and called the nurses daily for updates. On the weekend, they were further dismayed to receive a telephone call from Franny requesting that they not visit.

During the second weekend of Franny's stay, the Thompsons were asked to come and visit so they could attend a family session, which was a required part of every girl's stay at Brookton. As Ruth and Matt sat in the lounge waiting to be admitted to Franny's unit, groups of girls passed by on their way to meals and activities.

"I was struck by how many of them were complaining about their parents, and consoling each other because they would 'have' to go on a pass with their mother that weekend. One girl even said 'I'll be there for you when you get back!' to a girl who was scheduled to have lunch off grounds with her parents. I simply couldn't believe it!" Ruth said, her voice breaking.

As they waited for the therapy session to begin, she felt trapped, locked away from her daughter and placed in a "no-win" situation along with Matt. The communication she'd had with Brookton had already made her feel defensive, and now she suspected there would be more of the same. No matter what she or her husband said about what they perceived to be Franny's normal childhood and functional family, they were destined to look either oblivious or dishonest.

The family session turned out to be as bad as anticipated. Ruth was thankful she'd relented at the last minute and allowed Cliff to stay with a friend while they made the trip. Having him involved in the hour of therapy would have been harmful.

The therapist had taken a family history from Franny, and used this as the basis of the session. She reviewed the "many times" Ruth had encouraged Franny to take dance lessons, and the fact that Franny had been forced to stay on the dance troupe even when she wanted to quit. (In reality, Ruth had prepaid for a year of lessons and since there was only a month left when Franny decided to quit, she wanted to finish out the contract.)

Ruth had also reinforced her daughter's poor self image by comparing how slender she was and how big Franny was. (Again, Ruth pointed out that what she had commented on was the fact that she was short, like her sisters and mother, while Franny was tall, like Matt and his family.)

Matt, on the other hand, was chided for not being more involved in his daughter's life. While he frequently took Cliff on camping trips, he did nothing with Franny. The therapist wasn't moved when Matt informed her that Franny had been invited on every camping trip, but refused to go.

"See what I mean?" Franny interjected. "He deliberately picks things Cliff likes to do so I won't go along."

The visit to Brookton, eagerly anticipated by Ruth and Matt, ended with a mostly silent return trip home. Neither of the Thompsons felt reassured after spending time with Franny, but the director of Brookton felt their daughter was making progress. Their recommendation was for another two weeks at Brookton, and then a month long stay at Brookton Village, an aftercare program.

Brookton Village, which the director called "residential care," would allow Franny to live in an apartment type setting with four other girls and a counselor around the clock. She would meet daily with a tutor to do schoolwork, prepare meals with supervision, and attend daily therapy sessions back at Brookton. Most of the cost of a stay at Brookton Village (in the range of $40,000) would not be covered by Matt's insurance.

Once they were back at home, Ruth called Dr. Wells and Nick. Still struggling not to cry, she told them about the therapy session and the suggestion that Franny go to Brookton Village. Both the doctor and Nick responded with sympathy, but didn't advise going against the recommendation made by Brookton's medical director.

Matt's father volunteered to provide the cost of a stay at Brookton Village, so Franny was discharged to there after a month at Brookton. Ruth and Matt visited every weekend, noticing that their daughter seemed to be improving, and that her attitude toward them had softened noticeably. By the time she returned home, her binging/purging was reduced to once or twice a week, and her cutting had stopped. Ruth remembers an appointment with Nick shortly after Franny's discharge.

"Please forgive me!" she begged, hugging her mother tightly. "I know you and Dad have always been there for me. I'm so sorry for being so awful to you."

Franny continued to make slow progress toward recovery, and frequently told both Matt and Ruth how grateful she was to have parents like them. During one of their periodic "check-ins" Nick let them know they weren't the only family whose daughter had gone through a "parent hating" stage during inpatient treatment. He'd just returned from a professional conference where there had been a hot debate about the philosophies used by different treatment facilities.

"Some therapists think that you have a better chance of success if you find a 'cause' for the eating disorder. Parents are an easy 'cause,' and one you can probably change. Others, like myself, focus more on what's happening right now, and what purpose a girl's eating behaviors accomplish for her," Nick told them. "As you can imagine, there were strong feelings about the benefit of each approach, and unfortunately, neither side had any hard data to support its success rates. Brookton and places like it screen out the really complicated cases, and only accept girls with families who are involved and supportive, so of course their outcome statistics look great.

But if they took in everyone with an eating disorder, and really focused on long-term behavior change, I bet it would be a different story."

The care required by the children whose parents I spoke with ranged from completely outpatient to much more intensive inpatient. There were relatively few children at either end of this continuum, with most clumped somewhere in the middle, needing a mix of mostly outpatient and episodic inpatient treatment. Some examples of each include:

- A boy who was receiving no care until he entered an intensive outpatient program. (Only one boy in these interviews had ever been hospitalized)
- Two girls living at home but attending outpatient programs that specialized in eating disorders that required daily attendance
- One girl who was inpatient at a residential eating disorder facility
- Two young women who were chronic and receiving long term care in group homes. Both of these children had gone through dozens of inpatient treatments before being placed on public assistance and surrendered to the care of the states they lived in.
- Many of the girls and one boy who had recovered continued with occasional outpatient therapy in the form of visits to a counselor and/or medical doctor

When more intensive care was required for a child, there were a variety of options used. Most often, the type of inpatient care selected focused specifically on eating disorders, but a few girls, like Franny, were treated in the medical or psychiatric units of a community hospital, at least initially.

In general, the options for treatment include:

Intensive outpatient program: This involves more therapy than a child would normally receive, for example three to five sessions a week. There are usually other therapies involved such as nutritional counseling. These programs are designed to offer a child support for several weeks.

Day treatment or partial program, also called a partial hospitalization program: This is a structured program where treatment is offered for part or all of a day, and the child then returns home for night. School lessons, nutritional supervision, and family therapy sessions are often included. Participation in a partial program is typically a month, more or less.

Community hospital or medical center: This treatment is considered acute care, and will mean the child stays in the hospital around the clock. There are two options (assuming both are available). The child could be on a medical unit if he or she is medically unstable and if there is a need for cardiac monitoring, IV fluids, or NG tubes. If a child is suicidal or in danger due to the eating disorder, he or she could go to a psychiatric unit. Sometimes, a child will go to the medical unit until stable and then be transferred to the psychiatric unit. Some community hospitals have a special inpatient eating disorders unit or program, either as part of their psychiatric unit or separate from it. Depending on the particular problems he or she experiences, the stay will most likely be short.

Psychiatric hospitals offer only psychiatric care: There may or may not be an eating disorder unit within the psychiatric hospital, but a child will need to be medically stable before he or she is admitted, but still "acutely ill" meaning suicidal or in serious danger from the eating disorder.

Inpatient Eating Disorder Facility: This kind of care encompasses a wide gamut of resources, from a homelike institution with nurses and therapists where patients live and receive treatment for an extended period to a dedicated apartment where patients go to live under supervision and learn to gradually assume responsibility for their daily activities. If the facility provides a more intensive level of medical care and is accredited by JACHO (Joint Accrediting Commission for Hospitals and Organizations), care may be reimbursed by the insurance company. If it offers "residential care" which does not include intensive medical care, your insurance company may refuse reimbursement for the stay (or care provided).

Sometimes, visits to Emergency Rooms for care punctuated episodes of more formal care. One mother said: "We've had so many ups and downs with our son in the last two years. It seems like we've spent days at a time inside of ERs."

The emergency room was used for serious problems such as rehydration (IV fluids) or assessment to determine whether there was a medical or psychiatric crisis which needed impatient treatment. If a child was cutting and inflicted serious damage, an ER visit or evaluation was warranted, and in one case, a girl who began to vomit bright red blood while purging was rushed to the hospital.

Pluses and Minuses

As with other forms of care, inpatient treatment had both benefits and drawbacks. Often, this type of care occurred after a long struggle at home to help a child overcome anorexia or bulimia. Sometimes, it was terrifying for parents to "surrender" their daughters to inpatient care, which often meant restricted visiting hours and locked doors to keep patients from leaving. At other times, it was a relief to have more intensive efforts made to help the child.

Comments from parents about various kinds of intensive treatment include:

"We had to be separated. We were so codependent on each other. And she needed to start over from day to day, learn how to eat again and so on." [Daughter in residential care]

"During our time we always were told to do this and do that, and we did it. But then they would take away her privileges like phone calls and I think we paid more of a penalty than she did." [Daughter in eating disorder facility]

"We were so hopeful about [facility]. It was her first admission anyplace, and we were desperate to find a safe place that could deal with all aspects of her problems. Our insurance denied coverage but we couldn't go on with the behavior any longer, so we took her there. She admits that from day one she was just counting the days until discharge, and figured out how to get through the program....I too carry some feelings about the experience because they seemed too easily buffaloed by her...." [Daughter in eating disorder facility]

"I have tried to talk to men with EDs or read books, but I'm afraid there's not much out there in regards to boys" [Son who needs inpatient care, but cannot find it]

According to the parents I spoke with, there was no way to foresee the outcome of inpatient treatment. Some girls were so seriously ill they were hospitalized at the time of diagnosis, while others were able to avoid institutional care until much later in their illnesses. Here are some of the experiences:

A young woman who had been acutely ill with anorexia and bulimia for six years was hospitalized within a month of diagnosis and spent 80 to 90 days in the hospital. She has been in over twenty programs, sometimes for as long as 75 days. Her father says: "In some ways there's less stress when she's in the hospital because you know she's not going to die and you don't have to deal with her on a daily basis. The real stress comes from wondering what happens after she's discharged. After her first hospitalization they said: 'This is the easy part. The hard part is when you get home.' They were right."

Another girl who had been ill for three years was hospitalized for depression and an eating disorder. She had lost forty pounds in four months, so she was admitted to the psychiatric ward of a university medical center, and from there to an inpatient eating disorder unit. Because she was a teen and her home was far away, her mom was allowed to stay with her in the town far from where they lived. Gradually, the girl was allowed to go out for meals with her mom, and then to spend overnights with her mom.

Another teen lost twenty pounds in two months, but when the physician suggested hospitalizing her at a hospital distant from her family her mother refused. She feared her daughter's health would decline further in an unfamiliar setting, so she opted to have the child continue to be treated at home, with visits to a therapist and physician. Eventually, the daughter recovered.

Another mom whose sixteen year old was diagnosed with anorexia initially drove her to a hospital nearly four hours away once a week every week for nearly five months. Her daughter seemed to recover, but a few years later she ended up in the hospital after severe weight loss. When this occurred, the girl was terrified of hospitals because her therapist had led her to believe this was the worst outcome possible. Her mom stayed with her to allay her fears, but after discharge this young woman was quickly readmitted two subsequent times. After the third hospitalization, a residential treatment setting was suggested, which was another alternative the therapist had warned against. In reality, the facility her parents located was life saving for this girl.

Another girl who was hospitalized twice benefited from the experience. Her mother commented that in the hospital, her daughter was with other girls who wanted to recover, whereas at home her school girls didn't want to recover. Other parents commented on the "tricks" their daughters learned in the hospital, and felt any contact with other children who had eating disorders brought out an unhealthy competition.

A young woman who struggled with anorexia for ten years avoided hospitalization until she was in her twenties. At this time she became acutely ill but avoided a hospital and was treated for five months at a residential setting.

Another girl who was acutely ill did end up in the hospital, with an IV and on bedrest with a strict feeding schedule. She recovered temporarily but ended up back in treatment for seven months at a residential setting two years later. On discharge from that setting, she discontinued her medications, became depressed and resumed her anorexic behaviors again, leading to a 45-day inpatient treatment.

A son who began bulimic behaviors in high school became worse during his freshman year at college. When his parents learned he was severely restricting his intake and had lost a significant amount of weight, they made the three hour drive to his college and confronted him. He agreed to attend a clinic several times a week where he would work with a therapist recommended to his mother. This young man was able to stay in school and to begin recovery.

Another young man who had a seven-year history of bulimia was also attending college, experiencing phases of acute disordered eating and then longer periods of relative stability. He was not receiving any kind of inpatient or outpatient treatment and refused to consider it. (As noted previously, there was a clear difference in resources available to girls versus boys with eating disorders).

Inpatient Interactions

While children were in care, parents again talked about their frustrations with the treatment they received from doctors, nurses, and therapists who were, for the most part, strangers to them. One mom questioned the therapy her daughter received and asked the nurses: "For a girl so focused on her weight, why is she now in a place where they weigh her first thing in the morning, and determine the course of her day based on the weight?"

Another mom told me: "Take a bunch of girls who are focused on food and isolate them somewhere where meal times are the highlight of the day and all that is talked about is food, food, food, and it's a wonder anyone gets better."

Generic versus Specialized

There is a controversy over whether to use "specialized" (i.e., focused solely on eating disorders) versus general psychiatric (focused on a variety of mental health conditions) programs for inpatient treatment. One mother, whose daughter received extended care at a state hospital with a general psychiatric focus commented on the value of treatment that wasn't focused on eating. She says: "The day wasn't about food, and being with so many kids who had problems they couldn't change was a real eye opener for her."

Many girls (there was little information on boys) did seem to get better as a result of specialized eating disorder treatment. Even if improvement did not occur immediately, the process of recovery began during an inpatient stay. The parents of several of these young women credited that experience with "curing" their child.

Finding a Facility

The advice parents offered to others whose children needed inpatient treatment was not to assume that just because a place was famous or had a vigorous advertising campaign that gave it name recognition, it was appropriate for their daughter. Some who specifically inquired about the "success rates" Nick discussed, found that the numbers they were quoted only represented a small number of the women actually treated at the facility. For example, women who did not complete a full stay, or those who could not be reached at the time of the follow up post-discharge survey weren't included in the outcome data.

Most advised checking with other parents to see what their experience had been, and even asking the admissions counselors if they could speak with former parents. (Despite recent patient protection laws that may make this challenging, at least one facility has an arrangement in place that preserves confidentiality but offers to put prospective patients and their parents in touch with patients who have been treated there.)

RESOURCES

If you aren't sure of what resources are available in your geographic area, the best database I've found is at: http://www.edreferral.com/treatment.htm.

11
Battle of the Titans: Dealing with Insurance Companies

❧

"WE'RE SORRY TO INFORM YOU THAT YOUR PLAN ONLY
PERMITS COVERAGE FOR INPATIENT TREATMENT AT AN
ACUTE CARE FACILITY. THEREFORE, THIS CLAIM IS DENIED."
STATEMENT FROM INSURANCE COMPANY TO INSURED PARENT

Mickey Rand was a "frequent flier." Two years into her anorexia, this nineteen-year-old girl had gone through five extended inpatient stays, all of them at her local hospital where the nurses and doctors knew her by name. After the fifth time, Mickey seemed to have put her anorexia behind her, and had a plan for the future. Reluctantly, her mother Tina, a school teacher, and dad Bob, the manager of a home improvement store, agreed to send her to a college an hour away, filled with both fear and hope.

Mickey's anorexia "converted" to bulimia during her second year of school, which prompted her to begin seeing Eileen, a therapist at her college. She told Tina and Bob she was struggling, but she was okay. When she came home on fall semester break, she talked at length about her intention to kick her eating disorder once and for all. She also proudly presented her parents with her 3.8 GPA.

It was hard to have Mickey at home. Every night, Tina would hear her daughter in the kitchen, rummaging through the cupboards in search of food. The next morning, their fifteen-year-old son Todd wouldn't have any breakfast because Mickey had consumed the boxes of cereal Tina bought every other day. The kitchen was always a mess, filled with evidence of Mickey's bulimia, as was the bathroom.

"I'm not sure she's doing as well as she led us to believe she is," Tina said to Bob after Mickey had returned to school. "But to be honest, I'm glad to see her go. I wonder how her roommates put up with all that binging?"

Mickey checked in with her parents by phone and e-mail on a regular basis, still cheerful and upbeat about her classes and social life. It was a different story when she visited on holidays and some weekends. Despite an upbeat attitude, her binging behavior was like "a cloud of locusts going through the kitchen."

At the end of five long days of spring break, Tina blew up at Mickey about the vomit she found in the bathroom again and again. Mickey denied her binging and purging was as extreme as Tina suggested, and angrily left for school without saying good bye. Guiltily, Tina wondered how their family would live together in the summer.

Meanwhile, Bob was e-mailing his daughter regularly, begging her to get more help. "You really need to think about an eating disorder program. We'll find the money to pay for it if you'll agree to go," he offered.

Before the Rands could decide how to survive the month of June financially (a typical binge cost fifty dollars for one weekend) or emotionally, Mickey announced she had decided to stay at school for the summer. She intended to earn tuition money by working as a research assistant, and stressed she wanted to be close to Eileen so they could continue therapy. Somewhat relieved that their daughter was at least committed to therapy, her parents agreed with the plan.

Midway through the summer, Tina was at her job as a summer school teacher when she was summoned to the phone by her worried secretary. The caller was Mickey, crying hysterically.

"I can't take this any more!" she sobbed, barely understandable. "My life is hell." For fifteen minutes, she told Tina her binging was now out of control, and that she was broke because of food. She had also begun cutting herself, and was worried that she would go too far.

Swiftly, Tina told her to go to her apartment and she would be there to get her in an hour. When she arrived, she found her daughter curled on the sofa, her face swollen from crying. Angry red gashes lined the tops of her thighs.

Eileen agreed to an emergency meeting with Tina and Mickey. At that session, she said she had been encouraging Mickey to consider an inpatient stay for the last three months, but Mickey adamantly refused, determined to recover on her own.

Now she appealed to Tina: "Mickey really needs more help than I can give her. Maybe you and your husband can convince her to go for an inpatient stay."

Mickey sat silently as her mother and therapist talked, but finally interrupted to say she was resigned to being admitted somewhere for more intensive treatment. Tina lost no time in obtaining Eileen's recommendations, and began dialing treatment centers on her cell phone during the drive home. She discovered that although their insurance company had never balked at paying for hospital care, both refused to pay for care at an eating disorder center. They called such care "residential" and said that because Mickey was not medically unstable, it wasn't a covered service.

Driving down the Massachusetts turnpike, Tina felt her voice breaking with desperation. She asked the person on the other end of the phone (who refused to share her full name) what she could do to get help for her daughter. "Take her to an emergency room and get her admitted to a hospital" was the response.

Bypassing both insurance companies, Tina called treatment centers directly and was told a one month stay, which they typically recommended, with a week of partial outpatient care would cost them $50,000. Knowing only that the therapist thought this place could help their daughter, Tina and Bob took out a second mortgage on their house so Mickey could be admitted. The next week, their daughter was in the treatment center.

The center offered a package of services that addressed Mickey's needs in a way the hospital stays had not. As she worked with the nutritionist and therapist, Mickey began to believe she really could overcome her eating disorder. For the first time in months, she felt optimistic about the future. When the center's doctor suggested a mild antidepressant to overcome her obsessive thinking about food, she agreed, and was amazed to discover her outlook completely changed by the time of her discharge from the center. For the week after that, she religiously attended the partial program, and then tapered into biweekly sessions with Eileen, and weekly support group sessions back at the center.

Tina and Bob didn't regret taking on the expense of their daughter's treatment, but they were angry with their insurance companies for denying coverage. They consulted with the Massachusetts Mental Health Advocate for advice on how to file a claim to force their carriers to pay health care benefits. (Although Bob's insurance was primary, the payment for benefits was usually covered in part by both companies).

For six months, the Rands exchanged hostile letters with their health insurance companies, and Bob called several times to speak with the claims adjuster, her manager, the Human Resources benefits adviser at the post office, and the mental health advocate. After these communications, he would look so broken Tina would fear for his health, but he was steadfast in telling her no matter what happened, Mickey's health was the first priority.

One of Bob's coworkers had a brother who was an attorney who worked in specializing in health care law. This coworker made a casual inquiry and returned to work to inform Bob that he could sue the insurance company for bad faith because they had failed to provide benefits Bob was entitled to.

Bob telephoned the attorney, who drafted and sent a letter to an administrator in the Claims Department and the Human Resources department of Bob and Tina's employers. After several exchanges between the attorney and the insurance company, a check for $50,000 arrived, enabling the Rands to pay off their second mortgage.

Although parents may have mourned the "loss" of their child to an eating disorder, their anger with insurance companies for denying care that could be life saving was equally intense. Although Bob and Tina's experience was typical, some parents experienced even worse treatment at the hands of what one dad called "heartless bastards." Said another father: "Some kid one year out of college would routinely refuse to approve the care suggested by a psychiatrist who had known my daughter for years."

Other parents found themselves spending even more of their own money than the Rands, without subsequent reimbursement. The top figure was $100,000, but most parents spent some of their own money on items that were not covered by insurance.

When a child's need for treatment became intense, an adversarial relationship between parents and their insurers quickly developed. Children who required care that was both medical and psychiatric found themselves in a state of limbo, denied coverage on both accounts. One father recalls being told that anorexia was a medical problem not reimbursed by his mental health carrier, but when he applied for medical coverage, the response was that eating disorders were psychiatric problems.

Some of the "tricks" moms and dads felt were used by insurance companies to limit coverage included: "They'll say they're going to pay for a month, then they'll pay for a half a month. You call and ask why they did it and they'll say, 'Oh, sorry, we don't know what happened there.' They play any game they can not to pay."

"My daughter was halfway through a recommended one month minimum inpatient stay at one of the best eating disorder facilities in the country. The insurance company refused to authorize the second half of her stay because they felt it wasn't medically necessary. Meanwhile the facility was calling us every day telling us she needed a new medication or more intensive therapy because she wasn't doing well. So what would any parent do? We put $16,000 on our credit card so she could stay, and paid it off bit by bit."

"Sometimes, we got it worked out, but not without a lot of stress. Other problems didn't get worked out which left us spending thousands of dollars of our own. Insurance companies always say no first, so you have to be persistent in going after them."

"We paid $10,000 for a one month stay at [an eating disorder center]. That was what <u>we</u> paid out of our pocket because insurance didn't cover it all."

"We discovered some kind of rule that there had to be ninety days between hospital stays — too late."

"Our son was denied coverage and dropped from our insurance because he was eighteen."

"All her doctors said she was on the verge of death, but our insurance company wouldn't authorize hospitalization because her vital signs were within the normal range. Her doctor finally got the okay to send her to the Emergency Room, and from there she was admitted because they wouldn't send her home. We've accumulated $10,000 in bills over that episode of care. We're still doing battle with the insurance company in an attempt to get it back."

"Medicaid covers most things but specialized stuff like vitamins aren't covered or protein drinks which cost a lot. Many other doctors (especially specialists) won't take Medicaid, and of course because she has been sick long enough to be placed on Medicaid she needs a very high level of care"

"I get a total of twenty mental health visits a year. Anything more than that I pay myself. Try and fix an eating disorder in twenty visits? No way." .

"There aren't a lot of resources out there to help you. One provider will say the girl needs a ED program, another a medical hospital, and the insurance first says it will pay and then it won't."

"When we were trying to get her eating again a nutritionist told us to keep food she liked in the house. We spend 50 to 100 dollars just to try and get her to eat."

"Initially they were good, but then we went out of network because she needed specialty care, that was a battle. Initially they denied then okayed, then limited sessions. It's been a constant battle to get treatment."

After such experiences, parents learned to fight back. Their suggestions for dealing with insurers arose from bitter experiences across the country:

• One mother mailed her insurance company an article on Anna Westin (http://www.annawestinfoundation.org/), a young woman who died after being denied coverage. Since Westin's parents sued Blue Cross/Blue Shield for an undisclosed amount (and won), the insurance company approved her daughter's treatment quickly.

• Like Bob, another father hired a lawyer to make threatening noises to the insurance company.

• A mother documented all of the care her daughter received during the first six months of her anorexia, and used this data to argue that no one at the HMO had the expertise to treat eating disorders. (She won.)

• From the beginning of her daughter's anorexia, another mother kept meticulous records of her daughter's weight, vital signs, and any diagnostic tests. When the insurance company argued that residential care at an eating disorders facility was not medically necessary, she faxed them a copy of her records to show that it was.

• Many parents suggested never sending an original copy of a receipt. Ask for two and keep one for yourself in case the insurance company requests an original and then loses it.

• Many states have Mental Health Associates who can help with thorny insurance issues. You can locate a list of these at http://www.nmha.org/affiliates/directory/index.cfm.

• The Center for Insurance Research (http://www.theworld.com/~cir/who_we_are.html) was used by one family. It's located in Massachusetts, but actually focuses on national insurance issues, and has a wealth of resources on its pages.

• Many parents empowered themselves through extensive reading, research on the Internet and information gathering from support groups.

• A parent had the leader of the support group make a call to the insurance company on behalf of her daughter.

Relevant comments from parents who had "taken on" insurance companies included:

"You have to be really smart and fight for services and push insurance companies and go through their appeals process, and know that's how it will get done. Here is my daughter dying, and this is what they made me go through to get treatment. I'm crying now because it's so frustrating and I hate it that this is what they do with mental health issues."

"It was a financial impact but not a hardship. There were troubles with the insurance company. Eventually they covered everything, but it took a lawsuit against the employer to force them to pay for what their obligations said they would pay for. You have to be persistent and insist on reimbursement because they can be pretty ruthless at times."

"My daughter was in a hospital that cost $1,000 a day. Insurance paid most of it, but that didn't compensate for time off work, food, parking, etc. Our fight with getting coverage went on for a year, eventually we hired a lawyer who was able to get the bill paid on our behalf."

"We had a hard time paying for therapy. In our desperation we went to people who didn't take insurance, and just wrote out checks. We were in such a bad place we would have done anything."

"Once my husband's parents helped us, but residential care is a problem because it is so expensive. Insurance companies said they wouldn't cover it, but we fought hard and found a bill in the California legislature that said it should be covered in California. They passed a law in 1999 that said mental illness should be covered like any illness."

"Play every game _you_ can. Pay half rather than all."

"Go to the insurance commissioner of your state."

"Buy the insurance plan offered by your child's school or college. In the end, it saved us."

"My husband's employer, a religious organization, put pressure on the insurance company to pay."

"Disability covers everything, it's wonderful."

"They pushed her out of the hospital after thirty days, which was probably too early. Residential wasn't covered, but we made a case for 'medically necessary mental health.' We have the Arizona Mental Health Advocate working to help still."

"They do it to wear people down. You really need to become your child's advocate and learn that you can't rely on the mental health system. Having a health care background or knowing someone who does is helpful."

"Our insurance was not helpful — when I needed help they couldn't provide referrals or tell me what they would or wouldn't pay for. My advice is appeal everything. Keep appealing. Change the system!"

Some General Legal Observations about ERISA

Virtually every insurance plan provides an internal appeal process and ordinarily this must be resorted to before the carrier can be sued. These appeal processes are never quick and – since the carrier decides who hears the appeal – successful appeals are the minority outcome.

A family's best legal remedy against an insurance carrier is a suit against the carrier for "bad faith" conduct. An insurance company owes its policy holders a duty of good faith. When that duty is breached and a carrier acts in bad faith the carrier can be sued for its bad faith conduct. Bad faith actions permit the plaintiff to seek an award of punitive as well as compensatory damages. Punitive damages can be several times the amount of compensatory damages; bad faith actions, therefore, provide real leverage against the arbitrary conduct of an insurance company.

Unfortunately, most families with insurance have that coverage through their employers and in the considerable majority of instances that insurance coverage constitutes an "employee benefit plan" regulated by a law called the *Employee Retirement Income Security Act*, better known as "ERISA."

Recent court decisions have indicated that ERISA, a federal law, pre-empts state law for bad faith conduct by insurance companies. In short, this means that the only remedy against an insurance company is the remedy set forth in ERISA. This requires, first, that the plan beneficiary follow the plan's internal appeal procedures. They are found in a document called a Summary Plan Description which must be given by the plan to each covered individual.

Only if the internal process continues a denial of coverage can the plan beneficiary sue for unpaid benefits. The plan has a significant advantage here; not only is it immune from bad faith allegations; it does not necessarily have to have been right in its decision denying coverage. It is sufficient that the Plan's trustees simply not have "abused their discretion." Thus the burden for Plaintiffs in ERISA cases is atypically burdensome.

This entire area of ERISA pre-emption of state law rights and remedies is controversial and subject to change. Families with significant potential liabilities for denials of coverage should consult a lawyer to see whether any practical relief is possible. However, they must remember that compliance with the plan's internal appeal procedure is mandatory and that failure to file a timely internal appeal may constitute a waiver of any right they might have to seek a remedy in court.

The lesson here is to read your policy or summary plan description carefully. Most eating disorder victims eventually run up high bills and parents, in addition to being caregivers, must to some degree become experts in insurance coverage. The law does require that insurance policies be written in simple and easy to understand language so that the typical family can understand their rights. Even so, the supposedly simple clear language in many plans can baffle even lawyers. If you don't understand plan language call the plan or your human resources department at work and ask for an explanation. Be sure to take notes and write down the name of the person you spoke with. This might be important evidence later if your problem with a coverage decision lead to legal action. *Source: Paul J. Dellasega, JD*

Help is on the Way

Every state has a mental health advocate whose job it is to protect the mental health rights of residents, and several parents were involved with activism around the legislation for mental health parity. As suggested, this kind of legislation is a way to "change the system."

The *Mental Health Parity Act* (P.L. 104-204) was passed by Congress in 1996 to create a federal mandate for treating mental health problems. It basically required that companies with more than fifty employees end "caps" on mental health coverage. Employers have found ways around the law by creating restrictions on mental health <u>benefits</u> (*i.e.*, limited numbers of visits or days of inpatient care.) In addition, some states have created laws that limit parity to specific mental health problems, thereby excluding several disabling conditions, like eating disorders.

In the end, Mickey Rand ended up getting the treatment she needed. Her progress toward recovery was priceless to her parents, but they were frustrated by going into debt because Bob's employer failed to provide benefits that the family was entitled to. Tina pointed out that had specialized treatment been substituted for the multiple hospitalizations that insurance happily reimbursed, recovery might have come even sooner.

The Rands, like so many other families across the country, are glad to do whatever they can to help their child survive and recover from an eating disorder. All too often, families pay a needlessly heavy price because a point is reached where family care is not enough and other resources they believed to be at their disposal are needed.

The hard dollars families are often forced to spend in these circumstances can eventually be earned back, but the residual frustration of being denied a benefit they worked long and hard to guarantee is not so easily offset. For some, the psychological "cost" of fighting for a benefit they believed was automatically guaranteed left mistrust and bitterness toward insurance companies that might never go away.

RESOURCES

For more information on mental health parity check:

http://www.nmha.org/state/parity/index.cfm
The National Mental Health Association website.

http://www.dearshrink.com/mhparity.htm
The Mental Health Parity bill died in the Senate in 2004. To read newspaper articles that provide further information, go to this site.

http://www.cms.hhs.gov/hipaa/hipaa1/content/mhpa.asp
This page provides a good discussion of the act in easy to understand language, and has a link to "Consumer Questions."

STATES WITHOUT PARITY AS OF 4/25/2000

Alabama

Alaska

District of Columbia (Has 1997 law mandating that there be MHSA Benefits in group, individual, HMO and state employee plans).

Florida

Idaho

Illinois

Iowa

Kansas

Massachusetts

Michigan

Mississippi

New York

North Dakota

Ohio (but the state does have parity plus for state employees for 1995-2000; FFS and employees have had parity plus since 1990, according to Roland Sturm, RAND).

Oregon

Washington

Wisconsin

Wyoming

From http://www.bazelon.org/issues/insurance/parity/2000statedata.htm#
Bazelon Center for Mental Health Care website

12
Higher Education: Involving Schools, Colleges, and Communities

ॐॶ

"I'M A TEACHER, SO YOU CAN IMAGINE HOW IT FELT TO HAVE MY DAUGHTER OUT OF SCHOOL FOR A SERIOUS PROBLEM LIKE ANOREXIA. IT WAS LIKE LIVING IN A FISHBOWL." *MOTHER/TEACHER WHOSE DAUGHTER WENT TO THE SAME SCHOOL WHERE SHE TAUGHT*

Teresa was thirteen when her eating disorder began with a sudden and severe food restriction. At first, she told her mother Sydney she wanted to become a vegetarian, but soon she eliminated other foods she had normally enjoyed from her diet: pizza, desserts, and any kind of snack food. Suspecting that Teresa had anorexia, Mrs. Marsh turned to the middle school where her daughter was a student for help. She called Sandy Carson, the school nurse, confided her fears about Teresa, and asked for advice on what to do next. There was a long silence on the other end of the phone.

"Mrs. Marsh, I'll try and find some resources to help you, but I simply haven't had to deal with this issue before," Sandy finally stammered. "We don't have any girls here with eating disorders." A few days later she called back with the name of an emergency telephone resource center Sydney had already contacted.

Over the course of the next year Teresa was diagnosed with anorexia and sent to an eating disorder center specializing in treatment of younger girls with eating disorders. At the center, a tutor assigned to help Teresa reported that his calls to the school for her assignments went unanswered. When Sydney went in person to ask the school for Teresa's work, the guidance counselor responded by giving her contact information for each teacher. Over the course of a day, Sydney telephoned each one.

When she called Teresa's English teacher, the voice on the other end of the phone was cold.

"I'll be honest with you, Mrs. Marsh," the teacher said. "I don't believe in coddling children who aren't really sick." Clearly reluctant, the woman quickly dictated a list of assignments.

Choked by tears, Sydney wrote down the information and then called her husband Neal at work to tell him what had happened. Neal was so furious with the teacher and the lack of support he felt they had received from the school he called his best friend, Alan, who was an attorney.

What he discovered amazed him. "Every school is required to accommodate disabilities," he told Sydney a few days later. "If we can get Dr. Blake to write out a statement saying Teresa is disabled, the school will need to respect that and work with us."

Teresa's pediatrician, Dr. Blake, provided a letter as requested, but instead of becoming more cooperative, the school officials were curt. They informed Neal they couldn't possibly make exceptions for every child in their school who had a psychological problem.

By this point, Teresa had returned to school, but was doing poorly again. The Marshes anticipated she would soon require another hospitalization if something wasn't done to help her.

Neal had done some research on the Internet and discovered that schools in other states had developed a coordinated program during the school day to support girls with eating disorders. The next morning, he faxed a letter to the school requesting that support services such as monitored meals and regular check-ins with the nurse or guidance counselor take place. Within a day, he had received a fax back denying his request due to a severe teacher shortage.

Teresa was too weak to continue attending classes. While she genuinely enjoyed her classes, she didn't have the stamina to walk from one end of the building to the other with a heavy backpack of books. She missed one week, then two of school. Dr. Blake saw her regularly during that time, and sent regular medical excuses to Teresa's guidance counselor. Since the insurance company wouldn't approve inpatient treatment for Teresa, the Marshes could only care for their daughter at home, supplementing their day to day interventions with visits to the therapist and medical doctor.

Neal was stunned when he received a citation at work charging him with truancy because Teresa had missed so many days of school. He called Alan and was able to get the citation taken care of, but the mental anguish it caused made him decide to bring a lawsuit against the school district for denying Teresa her rights. He asked Alan to send the principal a letter informing the school of his intent. The same day the notification arrived the school superintendent called Neal at work and apologized for what he said was "a serious misunderstanding." He quickly made arrangements for Teresa to have a school district tutor come to her home each morning, and Sandy attended some conferences on eating disorders so she could develop a specific program for their school. By the time Teresa returned to classes, five other girls had joined the program, which consisted of eating lunch in a special area of Sandy's office suite, and an afternoon support group with the guidance counselor.

Neal dropped his suit against the school, and the day Teresa "graduated" from middle school she took flowers to thank Sandy for all the support she had come to provide. The Marshes say they have put the incident behind them, but they still speak disparagingly of a school system that they feel ignored a major problem among girls in the hopes it would go away.

Since the young women and men described in this book were at varying points in life (i.e., high school, college, or graduates) not every family had to interact with schools or employers to ask for support (employers are also required to accommodate disabilities). Sometimes families preferred to keep the eating disorder of their child a secret, and did anything they could to prevent their schools from discovering why their children were absent or functioning poorly.

A Different Kind of Learning

When there was a need to become involved, working with middle or high school administrations because a child was still legally required to attend classes was a different experience from interacting with colleges, where students were technically adults, and could withdraw on their own. In the few instances where employers needed to be involved there seemed to be a general willingness to try to help the ill child with whatever accommodations were needed.

Sadly, the response given to the Marshes was all too common for parents with children still in school who did make the problem known. One parent was specifically discouraged from pursuing an independent learning plan for her daughter because that might create a "stereotype." Another mom said the school wanted nothing to do with her daughter's eating disorder, and was clearly not going to help either her or the mother.

When girls had health needs that required coordination with the school or required homework assignments as Teresa's did, parents had no choice but to talk with teachers and counselors. The responses were mostly negative. Says one: "The people we dealt with at school seemed to think girls with anorexia are in the same category as kids who smoke pot or drink beer, that you just slap their hands and tell them to stop. Schools think they know about eating disorders, but they don't. Even classmates and friends don't really understand."

The mom of a girl in private school shared her experience: "When I called the director, he asked me not to talk to other parents, or let them know what was going on. I got this sense he thought anorexia was contagious, and didn't want parents worried."

Another commented: There was an almost public shunning of my daughter [by adults], as if she had done something so wrong no one wanted to be seen talking to her."

The Up Side

Not every school was unresponsive. Another pair of mothers discovered a virtual "epidemic" of eating disorders when one of their daughters became anorexic. They promptly went to the school and demanded intervention because they saw girls reinforcing each other's behavior. They were successful, and the classroom sessions on eating disorders that were implemented because of their advocacy seemed to help others. In other cases, schools worked cooperatively with parents to meet educational needs, and school nurses like Sandy and guidance counselors provided direct help to children who needed support during the school day.

Says one mother: "It took many letters and fighting, but I cannot bear to see another mom go through this. Eventually I went to the Board of Directors and asked for a speaker to come in and talk about eating disorders. Now the school focuses on healthy eating, and damages that can occur by not eating healthy."

Another mother shared that her daughter, now recovered, had taken on a program to educate younger girls, and regularly visited the schools to talk. This was both a reinforcing experience for her daughter, and an effective prevention strategy for middle school students in the mother's opinion.

Teacher Education

Teachers had the potential to be allies in the battle against eating disorders, and sometimes were. When one teacher called a parent to ask about a daughter, the parent actually appreciated it and didn't consider it intrusive. More often, parents expressed disappointment when their children's teachers didn't take a more active role in informing them of what was going on during the school day. Since many times it was friends who noticed at school that disordered eating behaviors and/or excessive exercise were occurring, parents felt schools should be more proactive, and should have a response plan ready when students struggled.

Girls found mealtimes at school difficult, and many parents had to devise strategies to overcome their children's fear of being observed eating. Some compensated with larger breakfasts and after-school snacks, and others arranged for their children to eat in a classroom or private location. Like Sandy, one school nurse offered girls the option of eating lunch in her office with her.

Working Together and on Your Own

If a child's activity needed to be restricted, parents were often the liaison between the child's physician and the school, and had mixed feelings about how the situation should be handled. In one case, being "different" from her peers and having to stand on the sidelines during gym class helped a girl move toward recovery, but in other situations families didn't want their children's illnesses made so public.

One high school student who loved school was desperate to keep her life as normal as possible, so her parents used being in school as incentive. As long as she reported accurately what she ate and maintained her weight, she was allowed to attend; otherwise she would be homeschooled. Her mother, a school teacher, chose not to tell the school her daughter was anorexic because she felt there would be negative repercussions.

For the affected child, parents identified other problems when being out of school for treatment. One young woman went back to school to find that her best friend was no longer her friend, and never got back on track with her class. Another girl returned from inpatient treatment and found that her classmates who continued with disordered eating habits were a bad influence on her.

One parent pointed out the tremendous influence schools in general have on children. "My guess is that eating disorders are caused as much by the environment outside the home as the environment inside the home. When your kids spend as much time at school as at home, I think you should learn as much as possible about what goes on at school, and what the school can do to help. It's at least as important as therapy," one father advised, questioning whether his daughter's relationships with friends influenced her eating disorder.

Two mothers shared detailed stories of daughters whom they felt developed anorexia in response to teasing or other negative comments or behaviors of their peers, and this was clearly the case with boys. (Studies have shown connections between eating disorders and relational aggression, which is the use of relationships rather than fists to hurt another.)

Anorexia U

Early in my teaching career I was surprised to find the words "Please STOP barfing in here!" scrawled across the bathroom door across from my office. Now, after nearly two decades of working with young men and women, I would feel sad rather than shocked in response to that message.

As illustrated in previous chapters, eating disorders are rampant during the college years. My own experiences as a professor at a large university underscore the stories parents told me about their children: binge and purge sorority parties seem to be an acceptable pastime, sports teams can exacerbate tendencies toward eating disorders, and the general stereotype of weight gain during the first year away from home can trigger many.

One girl whose eating disorder was discovered and treated while she was at college admitted to her parents that bulimia had been a problem for her since a very young age, but leaving home caused it to flare out of control. When this young woman's best friend pushed her to go for counseling, she was pleasantly surprised to find the infirmary had a treatment program already in place for students.

In another situation a roommate noticed binging and purging behavior and called the child's parents. Although it was beneficial to receive this information, the parents were surprised no one else had noticed something was wrong with their son.

One father whose daughter had to withdraw from college because of bulimia found the school's cooperation a relief. Although it didn't suggest any therapy or help specific to eating disorders, he recalls that it did refund the whole semester's tuition without challenging him.

On the Job

Employers seemed equally helpful when working with adult children who had a need to take time off for treatment. Many assured the job would be available when the adult child came back, and some accommodated work to the child's needs.

Schools and bosses were similar to therapists in that they were an integral part of a child's life, and therefore had great potential to help a young woman or man overcome anorexia or bulimia. After hearing so many discouraging stories about the unhelpful responses of middle and high schools, I'm not surprised many parents and children want to keep eating disorders private.

The good news is that some institutions and employers were helpful, and recognized a need in not just one particular child, but every person with the potential to be affected by anorexia or bulimia. That's all of us.

Some General Legal Observations about ADA

To a parent, a child suffering from a severe eating disorder unquestionably has a "disability." While the Americans with Disabilities Act ("ADA") prohibits most forms of disability discrimination, and many states have similar laws modeled on the ADA, this law provides far less practical benefits for caregiving families than the FMLA.

In the employment setting the ADA applies only to employees with disabilities. It offers no benefit to the parents of disabled children. The ADA provides significant benefits to applicants for employment but this offers no protection to a 14 year old anorexic. As an anorexic child grows older and enters the job market or continues in higher education, they do enjoy ADA protections. The ADA is unusual in American discrimination law. Most such laws are interpreted broadly to protect an individual from race, gender, or age discrimination, etc. For the disabled, however, the courts have narrowly interpreted what constitutes for legal purposes a "disability" and most eating disorder victims would probably not be considered "disabled" although they might enjoy ADA protections if the employer or school treats them as individuals "perceived" to be disabled although their disability does not meet the strict legal standards created by the courts.

A "perceived as disabled" anorexic or bulimic cannot be discriminated against because of that perception. The courts, however, are split on whether a "perceived as disabled" person is entitled to a "reasonable accommodation" – the most significant benefit for the disabled provided by the ADA.

Source: Paul J. Dellasega, JD

Section Three:

❧❦

Finding a Way

13
A Roller Coaster Life: Food Behaviors and Emotion Explosions

❧

"SHE USED TO HIDE FOOD EVERYWHERE SO WE'D THINK SHE REALLY ATE IT. I'D FIND THINGS UNDER HER BED, IN HER CLOSET, YOU NAME IT." *MOTHER OF A GIRL WITH SEVERE ANOREXIA*

"IT'S REALLY HARD FOR THE REST OF US BECAUSE HE VOMITS AND DOESN'T CLEAN UP AFTER HIMSELF. AFTER AWHILE IT GETS TO YOU." *MOM OF A BOY WITH ANOREXIA AND BULIMIA*

If there was a word to describe Amber Gray before she developed anorexia, it was "sweet." As the youngest of three children and the only girl, she had always received special attention from her dad Jeff, who teasingly called her "his little bear" because she'd been so cuddly as a child. One of their favorite routines was the big bear hug he gave Amber every night at bedtime.

Amber's mom Peg was thrilled to have a daughter four years after her second son was born, and looked forward to many happy "Girls' Day Out" events with Amber. She and Amber had a relationship she describes as "the normal mother-daughter thing, occasional tiffs, but otherwise very close."

Amber attended church every Sunday, and her family regularly visited with both sets of grandparents, who lived nearby. On holidays, many of their extended family would gather for special meals and activities. Vacation every summer meant a week at the beach.

At age fourteen, Amber began to lose weight rapidly. Concerned about her health, her parents immediately took her to their family doctor, who recognized the telltale signs of anorexia: extreme weight loss, a perception of her body as "gross," and mild depression.

Everything changed the day of Amber's diagnosis. Jeff was afraid to give her hearty hugs as he had before, and questioned his wife, a nurse, on how to interact with their daughter. Out of fear for her daughter's life, Peg admits she became overly involved, attempting to bribe or berate Amber into eating.

Amber's brothers John and Jordon were baffled by the change in their "little sister" whose sunny personality had always brought out their protective side. Now, each pound Amber lost seemed to make her more miserable. She screamed at them for eating a particular slice of pizza with more cheese than the rest, claiming they were "greedy pigs." She demanded to control which television programs were watched at all times, since she spent most of the evening on the sofa, too tired to do anything else. One time Jordon drank a diet soda Amber had put in the refrigerator for herself and she flew at him in a rage, scratching his arm.

Peg took a leave of absence from work, afraid to leave Amber unsupervised at home after school. Some days were calm, with all three children climbing off the bus together and seeming in reasonably good spirits. Other days were horrors, with Amber shrieking in anger as soon as she came through the front door. More than once, Amber ran out of the house in the midst of an argument over food. One time when this happened during a blinding snow storm, Peg drove through the neighborhood in a panic until she found Amber twenty minutes later, nearly a mile from home.

Soon, the Gray family's mood revolved around Amber. When she had a good day, so did the entire family. When her behavior was difficult, each person withdrew, leaving Peg to handle her. Often, Peg was the target of Amber's negative emotions. Sometimes, the insults her daughter hurled at her were so hurtful she would take the phone into her bedroom and call Jeff at work, in tears.

Jeff remembers the three years of his daughter's anorexia as a time of constant tension, even when Amber was in a "good" mood. "She could change at the drop of a hat," he explained. "It was eerie."

In addition to dealing with rages, Peg was juggling Amber's multiple appointments with the doctor, therapist, nutritionist, and support group. She spent long hours sitting and waiting for the visits to end. In particular, she found it challenging to wait through the hour of the support group since Amber would always be upset afterwards if other girls had lost more weight than her.

It wasn't until Peg happened to talk to her neighbor Greta that she discovered other moms had confronted similar behaviors. Greta's oldest daughter had a three year struggle with bulimia, so she had gone through many of the same situations as Peg, and worse. She was able to empathize and offer suggestions on how to deal with both the mood swings and food focus. Gradually, Peg came to believe Greta's assertion that Amber's outbursts weren't reflective of her feelings for her mother as much as an outlet for her frustration over the eating disorder. It was still hard to be a target, but she became better at deflecting and even, on occasion, preventing her daughter's rages.

When your child develops anorexia, bulimia, or another kind of eating disorder, a complete transformation of his or her personality can occur, as happened with Amber. Sometimes, parents were frightened by these changes, and again echoed a sense of "losing" the child they thought they knew well. More than once, I heard the comment that parents felt as if their real son or daughter had "gone away," and would never again be the child they once knew. They said:

"I can't stand to watch her push food around on her plate, pretending to eat. Why not just admit she isn't going to take one tiny bite more than she has to? Our supper usually ends up with this détente, my husband and I waiting for her to finish, and her equally determined to limit her calories."

"He's so critical of other people and their weight, and how much they eat. At times he can be downright cruel, and I want to remind him of what he's doing to his body."

It's Not about Food

To cope with these feelings, one mother stressed the importance of understanding what Peg learned from Greta: *"Food behaviors are not about you."* She discovered that as soon as she began to take her daughter's refusal to eat or her anger over food issues personally she, too, became angry, which was counterproductive for everyone involved.

Anger and raging behaviors like Amber's were a "hallmark" for many children. The degree to which a girl could become out of control was terrifying to some parents. Boys did not seem to become as extreme as girls, although they acted in challenging ways:

"My son has two personalities. When he is at his worst, binging and purging or restricting, he is totally focused on food and won't talk to me about anything else. He also blows up easily and acts like a completely different person."

"He will lie or do anything else he believes is necessary to make us believe he doesn't have the problem anymore."

"He used self injury to control others. The more out of control life was, the more self injury he did."

During rages, often the child said cruel things about herself and those around her. More than one parent described their children as going "totally crazy." One dreaded trips back from an eating disorder clinic visit because his child was often upset within the confines of the car.

Fathers admitted that a child's fury was often contagious for them. They seemed to respond with more anger, and even disgust, than mothers:

"She definitely became angry and it was so bizarre because we were involved in her life like she was a two year old. When her nutritional status was low, she would almost always have temper tantrums and just be a mess."

"My life was a rollercoaster. I never knew what to expect because she was so belligerent and defiant. Sometimes I came home from work and it would be quiet, at other times chaotic.

I would get phone calls at work telling me to come home, she's having a meltdown."

"It was the rebellion that got to me. At one point, I completely disengaged from her and told her she would have to leave the house if I ever heard her use four letter words with her mother again."

These experiences sometimes led dads to a desire to physically punish their daughters to control unruly behavior. Two fathers admitted for the first time ever they struck their daughters in an attempt to defuse her raging. Of course, the physical approach didn't help either the parent or child.

To Weigh or Not to Weigh?

Although about half of the parents I spoke with delegated regular weights of their children to health care providers, others took responsibility for this at home. Many times this became the same sort of minefield as mealtimes, with daughters needing to be coerced and bribed to step on the scales.

One mother said: "Oh yes, we weighed her once a week until the time when she picked up the scales and smashed them against the floor and broke them. Now we don't keep a scale in the house for that reason."

Trigger Points

Several mothers commented on "triggers" of anger, noting that their daughters were not only riveted on food, but on their appearance, stopping in front of mirrors frequently to study their profile, examining photographs of themselves, and frequently commenting on the shape of their bodies. If any of these were perceived negatively (and they often were), it could set off a rage.

Like Amber, other children had behaviors which reflected their tortured relationships with food. These behaviors often created volatile situations that could then trigger a rage. Some of the things noticed were:

• Wanting to be in the kitchen constantly while food she wouldn't eat was being prepared
• Demanding to know the particulars of food preparation ("if butter touched it, she would fly into a fit and refuse to eat it")
• Becoming a vegetarian and then looking at every label for any meat content so she/he could refuse to eat it (common)
• Insisting on special "low fat" or "healthy" foods
• Having to measure everything eaten so she could control her intake
• Watching others eat when she wouldn't

In response to negative emotions that arose in these situations, a child's behavior sometimes involved throwing food (common), stealing money to buy food, and blaming mother for making her eat (common). While mothers and fathers couldn't always know what their children were thinking or feeling, outbursts or rages were demonstrations of anorexia or bulimia possessing their sons or daughters in an almost supernatural fashion.

What can parents do to deal with these behaviors? The ones I talked with used a variety of approaches, some which might work for one child but not another.

Here is a list of suggestions on how to respond to food behaviors. Note that some seem to contradict each other, or even the suggestions of "experts."

- Don't let the child help cook
- Put a time limit on table time
- Make food the child can't smash and break up
- Make plans for right after a meal so the child has to finish by a certain deadline
- Try not to focus on or talk about food
- Avoid confronting or plea bargaining around food
- Don't punish the child for not eating.
- Put an unflattering (emaciated) picture of the child on the refrigerator
- Prepare food the child will eat and keep it around
- Develop consequences for low weight
- Recognize that the child may relapse during times of stress
- Add things to the child's food to enhance caloric content
- Find "safe" foods
- Buy separate foods for siblings
- Make gradual changes
- Always eat together
- Provide any food the child wants
- Be firm and don't get engaged in debates about food
- Don't accommodate the child's food rituals
- Treat food like chemotherapy — the child must have it and there is no negotiating over the "dose"
- Provide a list of "must have" foods
- "I decided to buy an apartment sized freezer and lock it in my bedroom so at least there is some food in the house."

- "I won't let her starve to death, but I will only spend $10.00 per day on food. If she doesn't like it, or wants to binge and purge it, that's her choice."
- Hold the child accountable for food behaviors — don't let them remain secret
- Refrain from criticizing or belittling about food behaviors— be nonjudgmental and calm so the child realizes the illness doesn't need to be all consuming

For emotional outbursts, parents had these tips:
- Recognize that belligerence and hostility are related to the eating disorder
- Stay calm
- Try not to respond to the child's anger
- "Don't get mad back, which of course is easier said than done. Remember, it isn't really their anger at you, but anger over their situation."
- Present a united front as parents
- Don't leave the child alone
- Help the child feel safe
- Take all decisions out of the child's hands
- Find other ways to help the child feel good about herself or himself
- Help the child see that he or she is more than an eating disorder
- Start each day anew
- Recognize that sometimes you will respond better than other times
- "Parents have to deal with the anger, you really just have to put a bullet proof vest on because it's going to come hurling at you. Try not to take it personally."

- "You can't get into arguing with them — I always did and it never worked out, just wound her up more."

Take It as It Goes

Many of these responses were used by more than one parent atdifferent times, and sometimes, new strategies were developed as the child's needs changed. Moms and dads developed amazing expertise at defusing situations many professionals would find intimidating.

Sad or Mad, Equally Bad

Food behaviors and emotional explosions were not the only behaviors that challenged parents. Equally distressing were the signs of depression: withdrawal and extreme sadness. One parent quietly described his daughter's suicide attempt as a direct consequence of her bulimia: "She just felt desperate, and didn't know what to do. It seemed like the only way out to her."

Another father had a similar experience with his college-aged daughter, receiving a telephone call from the emergency room. He says: "We lived three hours away. As soon as we heard the news we got right in the car and drove down to the hospital. We couldn't get there fast enough."

Even less dramatic behaviors were difficult for parents. One mother recalls the month when her daughter seemed to spend the majority of every day in bed. One morning she came in and found her nearly catatonic, which finally prompted a hospitalization; having the situation addressed was actually a relief for her.

"The insurance company would say: 'Is she suicidal? Does she have a plan to hurt herself if she isn't admitted right now?'"

this mother shared. "What can be more harmful than lying in bed most of the day? But to them that wasn't serious enough. It took an almost complete shutdown before they would authorize treatment."

Several mothers and fathers noticed that their children were very depressed, but whether this began before or after the onset of the eating disorder was hard to tease out. Often, one parent remarked, an initial dramatic weight loss can give a child an initial "high" that might be followed by a let down, triggering depression and reinforcing the cycle of anorexia or bulimia. Withdrawing from friends and family because of the eating disorder was another cycle that was self perpetuating.

Changes that were occurring in the child's body secondary to food deprivation could also lead him or her to depression:

"I hadn't realized that when you don't eat you get lethargic and depressed. It makes sense, but until her doctor pointed it out I didn't understand that."

Another mother described the stress of seeing the enormous and painful burden her daughter placed on herself every day:

"She would up the ante every day. First it was eliminate snacks, then the next thing to go was breakfast, then meat. The pressure she put on herself was tremendous, and if she 'failed' in any little way, say taking in even 25 calories more than she wanted to, she would just try that much harder the next day."

Cutting (using sharp objects to harm oneself) was another behavior that many parents reported along with an eating disorder. This behavior was more common but not exclusive to girls, and seemed to occur in one of two situations:

(1) When the child was forced to eat and needed to "punish" him or herself.

(2) When disordered food behaviors weren't enough to satisfy desperate attempts to cope.

Cutting and self injury did not occur in girls who were suicidal, so did not seem associated with a desire to die, but rather was used as a tension release. Only one parent offered advice on how to deal with this, which was to ignore it, as she was told by therapists that commenting on it or reacting would reinforce it.

Consequences for All

None of the mothers or fathers interviewed had gone through an eating disorder themselves, but most found their own nutritional habits altered by a child's anorexia or bulimia. Sometimes this was for the better.

"We're all eating healthier," one mother admitted, describing how she and her husband and cut out red meat and made regular mealtimes a priority.

Others were less upbeat. "She watches every bite of food I put in my mouth," complained one mother.

Several frustrated mothers said they often felt like "The Food Police" in response to these behaviors and more than one said she gained weight during a child's eating disorder."I wanted to show her the world wouldn't end if she ate dessert," explained one.

If the descent into food obsessions and mood changes was dramatic, even more amazing to parents was the impact of adequate nutrition. If a child was able to resume and sustain a normal intake, moms and dads would receive what seemed like a miracle when the son or daughter who had seemed lost forever returned.

RESOURCES FOR FURTHER INFORMATION ON CUTTING AND SELF-INJURY

http://www/uwec.edu/counsel/pubs/selfinj.htm
From the University of Wisconsin's Counseling Services, this page explains self injury, offers techniques to overcome urges (distraction, communication, other forms of stimulation such as squeezing ice, finger painting, etc., exercise, soothing activities, lists of alternatives), and provides some additional resources.

http://sasisite.8m.com/SI.html
Self Injury website with a list of links to other resources and "A Letter to Self Injury."

http://www.geocities.com/FebruaryDove/urges.html
Fight the Urge website again offers alternatives to self injury (carry safe objects, keep hands and brain occupied, art, talking to a friend, list of emergency phone numbers, staying grounded, lists, snapping a rubber band against your wrist, identifying triggers).

http://www.focusas.com/SelfInjury.html
Definition of self injury including possible reasons for the behavior, how to get help, response of health professionals, and additional resources.

http://www.selfinjury.com/sifacts.html
S.A.F.E. (Self Abuse Finally Ends) provides statistics, types of self injury, treatment, and answers to other common questions.

http://kidshealth.org/teen/your_mind/mental_health/cutting.html
An informative article on cutting through the TeensHealth website.

14
Brothers and Sisters Who Hurt: Impact of Eating Disorders on Siblings

࿎

"SO HE JUST MOVED OUT. HE COULDN'T TAKE IT ANY MORE."
MOTHER OF A GIRL WITH ANOREXIA, REFERRING TO HER OLDER
SON

George was in fifth grade when his middle sister developed anorexia. Jen was three years older than him, and unlike his oldest sister Diane (a sophomore in high school), she spent time doing things with him like watching TV, playing video games, or just hanging out. He didn't notice anything changing about Jen until his mother Roxanne began to argue with her over dinner every night.

After a few weeks of this kind of tension at the table, George began to dread meals too. He noticed that Jen didn't seem interested in him anymore, or was downright irritable when he approached her. When he tried to talk to Diane about it, she said Jen was just a brat, and wanted to get attention for herself. All too often, Diane and Jen ended up in screaming matches too, usually over something stupid like clothes or belongings.

Over the next three years, George saw his sister admitted to hospitals and eating disorder facilities again and again. All too often, his parents were away in the evenings, traveling to see Jen during visiting hours. He was left alone with Diane, who continued to maintain that Jen was selfish and had become anorexic to punish her parents.

"Just wait and see. When nobody pays attention to her anymore, she'll stop," was all she would say when George asked her what was going on.

At this point, George wasn't even sure he knew what anorexia was. He knew that Jen refused to eat and was very thin, but lots of girls at his school were as thin or thinner than his sister, and no one was putting them in the hospital.

One time, for reasons he didn't understand, he had to go to family therapy with Jen, Diane, and their parents. The doctor asked him a lot of questions about his relationship with Jen, and he started to feel as if he was being blamed for his sister's anorexia. When Diane was asked the same kind of questions, she stormed out of the session and refused to return.

"Those doctors are a bunch of crazies," she told their mom, "And so is Jen."

When Jen was sent to a treatment center in another state, George's parents announced that everyone was required to attend a Family Week there. Diane threw a tantrum because it would interfere with her plans, but there was no negotiating. George dreaded going too, and felt embarrassed to tell his friends why he would be out of school.

At the center, there were several other families of girls with eating disorders. One of the brothers was George's age, but they didn't talk until an art therapy session, where both of them painted similar versions of the same pictures: their parents and sister together on one side of the page, and them on the other, alone. After that, George and the other boy spent every free minute together they could. They didn't talk about their sisters or eating disorders; both were just glad to have an escape.

"What's your biggest fear, George?" a therapist asked during a session with just their family. George swallowed hard before answering:

"I don't know what anorexia is, but I'm afraid Jen is going to die."

Both of his parents looked shocked when they heard this, and both of his sisters began to cry. In the minutes that followed, Diane admitted that she, too, worried constantly about Jen.

Family Week provided a turning point for George, and the rest of the family. The therapist sat down with him and Diane alone, and explained what anorexia was, and how it was treated. In another therapy session, the entire family discussed their shared concerns, and Jen tearfully apologized for causing such distress. Later, she would say it was the support and love of her parents and siblings that helped her recover.

The majority of the families I interviewed had two or more children in their family, which meant the eating disorder had an impact on siblings as well as parents. Regardless of whether the other children were older or younger, male or female, every parent agreed that anorexia or bulimia had led to a change in their lives.

All Kinds of Emotions

Responses of siblings varied as much as George's and Diane's: "My daughter [with anorexia] tried to turn her older sister against my husband and me. She would complain about us all the time, but her sister wouldn't have it. That drove a wedge between them that is still there."

"Her brother avoids it most times, but lately I notice he has snapped at his sister over TV which I consider normal sibling stuff. That's a sign life is returning to normal."

"I think there was some anger on his part, not understanding it and wanting her to just knock it off and stop getting so much attention."

"And so there was pretty much tension for us and our son never knew that tension until the eating disorder, and he hated it. I don't think he hated his sister, but he really felt that she was causing the family to blow."

"The whole school knew what she [girl with eating disorder] was doing, and that embarrassed my son."

"There wasn't any room for her twin sister's feelings. She didn't want to go to the hospital to see her sister."

"In the acute phase our son was very angry, and emotional and sad. He wouldn't come home because of his sister's illness."

"My husband, son, and myself lost sleep, lost weight, and had health problems due to stress."

At other times, the impact on a sibling was something as seemingly trivial as different foods at supper. One mother noted that her much younger son appreciated being served dessert as she worked to help her daughter gain weight, but another mother had the opposite experience:

"Whenever I came to the table with food my [teenaged] son would roll his eyes and comment on the skinless chicken or broiled fish, making sure I knew he didn't appreciate that kind of food. Sometimes he would stalk away from the table and refuse to eat anything. So that's how I ended up making two meals every night, one for all of us and one for my daughter."

Anger, confusion, and resentment were frequent responses of siblings. Often, initially, children of all ages were like George, and had trouble grasping the logistics of anorexia or bulimia. Parents would receive questions they couldn't answer, such as:

Why is [sister] refusing to eat?

What would make [brother] throw up everything he eats?

Is [sister] going to die?

Why are you always at the hospital/clinic/doctor's with [sibling]?

Life for the "Healthy" Kids

If the eating disorder was prolonged, as happened in many cases, siblings would sometimes become even more angry and resentful, like Diane, who was frustrated with both Jen's behavior, and the emotional drain she saw placed on their parents. Sometimes, parents would learn that the other sibling felt his or her feelings weren't as important as those of the child with the eating disorder.

Often, this anger would resolve, and the healthy brother or sister would come to try to support or help or even rescue their struggling brother or sister. Sometimes, the anger became transformed into grieving, as happened with one brother who became very emotional about his sister for a time, crying whenever her name was mentioned.

A younger sister received a lot of comments about her sister's bulimia at school, which bothered her terribly. She distanced herself from her sister for a while, but then came to realize how much she cared about her and reengaged in a polite relationship, but still says she must protect himself from being hurt by her. It's disappointing when she fails to recover, and when she is deep in her illness she often uses behavior hurtful to her sister.

At other times, siblings shifted between emotions, feeling both negative and positive toward the patient. One brother who seemed to be handling his sister's bulimia well ended up exploding verbally and accusing her of destroying their family and upsetting their mother. Later, he was contrite about his actions. Fortunately, when the sister recovered, he was able to forgive her and find pleasure in being with her and his family again.

Brothers were not the only ones who responded emotionally. In one situation, a "healthy" daughter, who had previously seemed to be coping, fled the house during a particularly tense incident where her sister and mother were arguing over food. This child refused to participate in family therapy, saying she felt like the "outsider" after one session. Again, with recovery came a renewed relationship with her sister.

In the case of a twin who watched her sister struggle with anorexia, initial anger dissolved into withdrawal. This sister eventually admitted that she was terrified about her sister's illness, so much so that it prompted anxiety attacks that sometimes interfered with her own appetite. However, she assured her mother that she did not have an eating disorder.

In a few cases, the sibling was the one person who was able to relate normally to the person with disordered eating.

One mother shared that it was her son who was often able to "talk his sister" down from unreasonable behavior and coax her into eating when she refused all intake.

Another shared: "It brought tears to my eyes because I know how hard it was for him to express how he was feeling, and he said: 'Sis, I know you're going through some tough stuff now and if you ever don't think you can tell mom or dad, you can tell me.'"

The Mature Sibling

When the healthy brothers and sisters were already adults it was still very hard to work out family relationships with them. More than one mother found it difficult to balance support for the disordered child with accountability to other children.

"How can we spend all this money on treatment that doesn't seem to be helping and deny my other daughter the wedding she always wanted?" lamented one interviewee.

Another adult sibling became estranged from his sister because of her eating disorder. To this day, his mother says they do not speak because she continues with her anorexic behavior, which he cannot tolerate.

For those siblings who were old enough, removing themselves from the house was a way to cope, so they did. One older brother chose to go far away for college to avoid witnessing his sister's anorexia. In response to his brother's bulimia, another brother chose to move into his own apartment to escape the smell. Another reason for avoiding home was the full focus of the family's attention on the child with the eating disorder.

Even when siblings were out or on their own, it didn't mean they weren't upset about the additional parental time and energy they thought their ill brothers or sisters received. In particular, one set of siblings chided their sister for the money their parents had spent obtaining care for her. The mother recalls: "We were in family therapy, and here they were, in their thirties, grown children, berating Anne for all the problems she had caused us. I think they were really just upset at seeing my husband and I so devastated and in so many ways by the anorexia and bulimia. But I began to realize that I <u>had</u> put Anne first, and that even though my son and daughter were grown with children of their own, they still needed me too."

How to Help

Parents suggested several ways of helping siblings cope with the eating disorder of a brother or sister. The first was to recognize that the bulimia or anorexia had the potential to impact on siblings in deep ways that might not be apparent initially. Anticipate that the healthy siblings will have needs of their own around the illness, and don't expect them to automatically cope without help was another piece of advice. It was also suggested that the parents make time to do things just with the healthy sibling.

A second strategy was to provide information about eating disorders to the siblings as desired, but in measured doses adjusted for age and developmental stage. Some brothers and sisters wanted to know all the facts, while others preferred not to. Offering the option of honestly discussing the status of the eating disordered child could sometimes provide an opening for parents to discuss the sibling's feelings as well.

Some parents suggested that protecting the sibling from the effects of anorexia or bulimia as much as possible was a good approach. This took place on a continuum that included allowing a child to be free from the environment by sending the healthy sibling to short or extended experiences outside the home (camps, clubs, visits to relatives, etc.). One parent saw her daughter's continual frustration with not having food on hand due to her sister's frequent binges and compromised.

"I bought some foods that were for [healthy sibling] only, and told my daughter she was absolutely not allowed to eat them. I also let [healthy sibling] keep snacks and food in her room, and even had a stash of goodies in my bedroom should we run out."

Family therapy was sometimes helpful in resolving dilemmas with siblings, but at other times siblings refused to go, and stayed distanced from the sessions. Parents thought it was best to accept this choice, and not to "force" a brother or sister to attend family programs.

Preserving routines, connecting siblings with others who had gone through similar experiences, and calling on relatives and friends to fill parental gaps that might occur were other suggestions made. Sadly, mothers and fathers often felt a struggle of conflicting loyalties when they had to both care for the eating disordered child and try to help the healthier siblings continue to function normally. On a more positive note, almost every parent noted that going through these experiences solidified the relationships within their families, and made them stronger than they ever thought possible.

15
A Day in the Life of a Parent

❧❦

"It was like a mantra in my head, "I can make her better, I can change this, it will all go away. But of course I couldn't and it didn't.""

"My sister looked at me and said, 'Just make her eat. It's that simple.' All I could do was shake my head and laugh at this insensitive comment, but that's my sister for you."

"We did what anyone told us. We didn't follow our own thoughts or intuition, we just obeyed."

"Connection with other parents, the 'been there, done that, got the tee-shirt' experience."

"We finally decided we had to go on with our lives, and take care of our other children, and ourselves."

Comments on what was stressful, and what helped

Responding to eating disorders from a parent's perspective is complicated. Love for your child causes anxiety and concern, while fear for his or her life can lead to anger and frustration. There are both emotional and practical "burdens" to deal with since a tremendous amount of day-to-day assistance is often required if the child is approaching or actually in a crisis.

During my communication with parents, I asked them to identify "the single greatest stressor" they experienced while caregiving for their eating disordered children. Almost everyone responded with a list of challenges, even when I pushed for "number one," so I decided to present a range of narratives in this chapter to better capture the diversity of situations.

Fear, Fear, and More Fear

By far, the most stressful aspect of an eating disorder was a parent's overwhelming concern that the child would die, or suffer permanent damage due to anorexia or bulimia. This fear was a constant, underlying day-to-day existence and becoming heightened during times of crisis. The mother of a boy with bulimia captures the feelings of many:

"Every time I look at him I wonder what is going on inside his body, and what kind of damage he is doing to it. Even if he recovered today, his abuse of his stomach has gone on for years. Sometimes he throws up several times a day... I can't believe how far downhill he goes, and my biggest fear is that someday he will die while vomiting. If that doesn't happen, I worry that something else related to his eating disorder will kill him. They [doctors] told me he could dehydrate himself or lose enough potassium by vomiting and go into heart failure, but when I call and say his binging and purging has become severe, no one seems to remember that.

I'm not like the boy who cried 'wolf' — when I get to the point of calling, I am concerned that he is in a state of emergency, but they don't take it seriously. So I go in his room at night to make sure he is still breathing, and still okay. I watch him during the day as much as I can. What else can a parent do?"

When parents watch children struggle so intensely, yet are unable to help, an emotional mindset occurs where parents can't switch out of "panic and powerless" mode. Even when the crisis is not acute, moms and dads live with the expectation that it could soon become so. Sometimes, the perception that a child can "control" his or her eating disorder and therefore end it adds an element of anger to a parent's fears.

An Ever Escalating Turmoil

In addition to fears about the child's health, parents experienced a combination of depression, guilt, helplessness, anxiety, self-blame, inability to concentrate, loneliness, and a constant sense of grief. In the words of a mother:

"When Carla was diagnosed with anorexia, my world changed forever. First there was my immediate feelings of failure: what had I missed, what had I done wrong in raising her, and how could I ever sit with a group of 'normal' mothers again and feel like a part of things? I suddenly saw myself as an outcast mother, and my beautiful daughter as a poor broken creature who couldn't be fixed. That was just the beginning.

Over time, I went through a variety of emotions: hopelessness was the worst. Until that point, I'd been able to 'fix' all the hurts and make things better for my children. Now I had this twelve year old, who used to snuggle on my lap when she was upset, too weak to get out of bed. The sense of worry and grief was nearly overwhelming. Even when I went to work, I would be tempted to call her school and see how she was doing, or I would be thinking about what I might make for supper so she would eat.

For reasons I don't fully understand, my husband felt we shouldn't tell anyone, so Carla's illness was our family secret. Our other children knew, but none of the relatives did. I finally confided in my closest friend, who has three grown successful daughters. She really tried to be helpful, but her comments made me even sadder. There were no happy times during those years of anorexia, not even the holidays or birthdays, because inevitably there would be a meal, and just as inevitably Carla wouldn't eat. She was so thin when you looked at her face all you would see were these big hungry eyes, reminding you of how bad she felt."

While parents never acclimated to the turmoil an eating disorder brought into their lives, they did begin to understand it, and to take steps to cope with it, as described in previous chapters. In cases where recovery still hadn't arrived many years later, mothers admitted they were still sad about their child (no father discussed this). To survive, they made a decision to accept the son or daughter's choice to remain eating disordered, and consciously focused their energy and effort on other aspects of their lives.

A Deep Sense of Loss

Parents' perceptions that their children had been "lost" to them was in many ways true. Not only had the son or daughter "left" emotionally but their appearances often changed so dramatically they were unrecognizable. Here are the words of a mother reflecting on the five years of her daughter's eating disorder:

"I had a dream for my daughter, and bulimia certainly wasn't it. Many of the milestones other parents take for granted are gone forever for us. There will be no prom, no graduation ceremony, no silly teenaged dates or slumber parties with friends — it all just fell by the wayside when Holly got sick.

She changed in so many ways: her smile was gone, her friends were gone, and her love of school was gone. When I looked at her, I barely recognized the girl who had been so cute and outgoing as a young teen. Instead, I saw this gaunt person whose hair was falling out and whose teeth were worn away. All those dental appointments I thought were so important were washed away by her constant vomiting.

Even when I talked to her, there was nothing I could connect with. I read every book I could find, but only got marginal help. The Holly I had known was gone ... and so was our relationship. I lost my mothering role and became the bad guy of eating disorders. [This mother's narrative picks up again as she describes her current feelings].

She is better, better than where she was a few months ago, and much better than she was a year ago. I should be happy, I am happy, but I can't help grieving the lost times, which we'll never get back. I'll never know what it's like to be the mom of a normal teenaged girl."

It was remarkable that dads did not report this sense of grieving as poignantly as moms, and this emotion was exclusively described in relation to daughters. Although parents again learned to live with this sense of loss and even to pick up with a healthy mother-daughter relationship when recovery occurred, there was always a tender place of remembering the many missed milestones.

The Un-Health Care System

Many aspects of the health care system were stressful, from the response of professionals to the money paid out of pocket for care. A father speaks for many when he summarizes the issues that he felt were most distressing for him. "It started with this cognitive disconnect. We were saying our daughter was sick, and they [unspecified health care professionals] were telling us no she's not. It was like a tug of war. Then we discovered that her therapist of one year knew that our daughter had an eating disorder and didn't tell us because Mandy wouldn't consent, but finally, everything came out in the open and the fun began.

I think I fought with insurance companies daily, and at one point thought I would have to sell my house to pay for her treatment. I could easily shell out a couple hundred dollars a week for her: over the counter anti-acids which she ate by the bottleful, Ensure or some other kind of feeding the doctor wanted her to have, the co-pay for medications and therapy, and then the food. She could eat through twenty dollars of food in one sitting.

I don't begrudge paying for the treatment things, but it does piss me off to think they [insurance company case managers] hear 'eating disorder' and automatically deny the claim. Then there was the ongoing question of whether we were doing the right thing. What did we know? The multitude of doctors we encountered each had their own different approach. Weigh her, don't weigh her. Make her eat, don't make her eat."

One mother spoke for many when she talked about her inability to respond authentically to comments made to her by professionals. A sense that she would appear as a "bad parent" drove many of her interactions with doctors, therapists, and nurses:

"There was also judgment of our parenting. What other situation can you think of where you would be expected to sit and listen to all the things you've done wrong for your child, but not be allowed to have any response or feelings to the accusation? What other situation would expect someone to take verbal abuse from professionals and then happily go home and provide loving care to a child who set up the abuse by what she disclosed or didn't? And what other situation would you find where you as a mother are forbidden to cry or show emotion because your daughter is so very ill?"

In addition to the emotional energy of negotiation and confrontation required to obtain care for a child ill with an eating disorder, the practical demands of providing care were stressful, and often provided primarily by mothers. One says:

"Initially, I was taking Carrie somewhere nearly every day of the week. We saw the medical doctor who monitored her vital signs and weight. That usually took two-three hours, all told. Then there were visits to the therapist who was seeing Carrie took another two hours. Sessions with the nutritionist so Carrie could make a meal plan and review the last week's menu were two more hours. The support group for her was three hours including travel. Some weeks, we had family therapy sessions, which was an ordeal for all of us, since we had to drive forty minutes each way to the office.

[There was a pause as the mother added up the hours and went on.] Those are just the things I did by appointment. I figure I spent twice that time buying food, making food, sitting with Carrie as long as it took to eat the food, and so on. Meals were a huge production at our house.

I spent a lot of time at the school, too, because Carrie had to be hospitalized and missed several weeks of classes. In the weeks before she was hospitalized and the weeks after she returned I still had to go in to meet with her guidance counselor and discuss how she was doing.

I don't begrudge any of the time I devoted to Carrie, it was worth it. What I do mind is the failure of doctors and therapists to acknowledge that you are the expert on your child. She is sick, and can't be expected to think or communicate clearly. Parents are the ones who know what's going on better than anyone else."

A father remarked on these kinds of activities, too, saying:

"It's like caring for an infant, we have to be at home for meals, schedule our lives around her, and constantly keep her safe."

Questioning the health care decisions they had made along the way tormented some parents. One mother recalls lying awake at night, reviewing her interactions with both her son and the health care system, and crying. A father confessed to being consumed by self doubt, still wondering whether the long ago choices he and his wife had made were the best ones.

Another health care stressor was the challenge to get help for adult children. Once a child turned eighteen (or even earlier), his or her consent was needed for treatment to occur. In my home state of Pennsylvania, the age of consent to treatment is fourteen, which created many problems for us. Regardless of the legal requirements, most professionals require the child's cooperation before they agree to provide care. This means it is virtually impossible to coerce a child into care until the illness reaches life threatening status.

One mother summarized the situation well:

"My sixteen year old daughter has gotten care as an 'in' and 'out' patient, but right now she refuses to seek any kind of help, which is terrifying me. Everyone who knows her keeps telling me to do something, to get her to a doctor or therapist, but what they don't know is I can't force her to do anything. I feel guilty about her illness and angry over her behavior, very conflicted, very torn."

Keeping Things Private

The isolation and loneliness many parents described because they couldn't share their "real" lives with others made them constantly on guard in their interactions with friends, family and coworkers. Many parents also reported feeling they couldn't act in a genuine manner or express their true feelings to their child, because they feared it might further exacerbate the eating disorder.

This mother's feelings are typical of those who kept the eating disorder secret: "My daughter Casey was mortified over the idea that I might tell someone she had anorexia. She strictly forbade me to talk to anyone, even her grandparents, about it, although I'm sure everyone who saw her knew something was wrong and wondered what kind of parent I was. No one questioned me point blank, thankfully, but many people dropped innuendos about Casey's appearance.

Add to that the fact that I could never say what was really on my mind to Casey. There was this censoring process: If I say this to her, will she react like that, or if I do this, will she think that? Sometimes when she became irritable she would scream the most hurtful things possible at me, and of course I could have screamed right back about how selfish I thought her behavior was, but I didn't.

In family therapy or when I spoke to her therapist, I heard again and again about all the 'mothering mistakes' I had made: being on a diet from time to time, being too strict so she felt overcontrolled, or being too lenient so she felt she didn't have boundaries. There was always feedback about me, and once when she was in a treatment center they said they thought it was best if I didn't visit because Casey and I had such a 'difficult relationship.' No one asked me if I <u>intended</u> to visit, or if I thought our relationship was 'difficult.' They listened to a girl who was severely underweight, malnourished, and depressed.

I was constantly on guard: one time I had an upset stomach when we visited Casey at the center and were asked to take her out for a meal. When I ordered soup instead of an entrée and passed on dessert, she jumped all over me about trying to lose weight.

My life became a life of secrets, hiding her anorexia from others, hiding my real feelings from her, and accepting all kinds of statements about my deficiencies and not responding back because then the therapist would be convinced I really was a hostile, defensive mother. Thank God my husband and I had a good relationship, and that he could always help me laugh — or at least smile — about the absurdity of the situation somehow."

Seeing the Signs and Symptoms

Watching a child consume thousands of calories knowing they will promptly be thrown up or seeing their sons or daughters refuse any food at all was a torment for parents, along with a host of other behaviors described in previous chapters. The list of overt food behaviors that were most distressing was long: rituals, hiding, vomiting and not cleaning up, preoccupation with food, refusing to eat with family, eating slowly, and eating all the food in the house. Several mothers commented on how difficult it was to hear their daughters vomiting through the bathroom door as they understood all too well the tremendous pressure on young women to be thin, and felt societal influences were part of the eating disorder.

In addition to food behaviors, other behaviors that appeared with the eating disorder bothered parents. These included: manipulation, sneakiness, dishonesty, negativity, nastiness, inflexibility, hostility, anger, and denial. The following synopsis of one mother and father's situation captures many of these issues.

"Lucy is our middle daughter; the other two are fine which makes us think this is just some kind of genetic screw-up. She got anorexia in her junior year of high school, possibly because an injury made it impossible for her to continue cheerleading, which was not only a physical activity but her identity.

After a year of restricting, she became bulimic and went in the opposite direction, so we've seen it all. When she was anorexic, it was painful to have a meal with her. She was so picky I often had to prepare special foods for her and a different meal for the rest of the family in the hopes she would eat. She'd chew her food forever and then spit it out into her napkin so she could feed it to the dog under the table, then she got to the point of just not eating at all.

Lucy never cared much about her appearance, but then she became very vain, and would often stare at herself in the mirror, turning side to side. Sometimes she would comment on how fat she was just so someone would tell her it wasn't true. She was super-critical of other women's bodies, looking them over and commenting on how heavy they were, even when that wasn't true.

We spent a fortune on clothes too, as her weight went up and down. With each new cycle, she would require a whole new wardrobe. When I started to protest, her therapist said it was a good way for Casey to 'express' herself, so I gave in.

When she went into an eating disorder hospital, she actually 'learned' new tricks on how to limit her intake. We later found out what a big joke it was among the girls: here they were, obsessed with food to begin with and now in a place where they got weighed every day and were given permission to count calories! At one point when we visited there she actually told us all the new 'tips' she'd picked up. Those things just spur a girl on, because the eating disorder is a weakness that gets reinforced and can only survive with attention. It was very distressing.

The bulimia was worse, though. There's something that seems almost immoral about it, wasting all that food. There was never anything to eat in our house because Casey ate it all. One time, we put locks on our cupboards and refrigerator at her request to try and limit her intake. Ironic, huh? For a year we pushed food, then we suddenly needed to limit it.

The stressor that stayed constant was her behavior. Of course she was very depressed — we've heard that most girls are. Seeing her so sad was torture, because nothing made her happy. All of her joy in life was gone. Even though she focused on food, she didn't even really enjoy that.

She also got manipulative — she could convince her doctor or therapist of anything. One time she had her [therapist] call the doctor and say Lucy didn't need to come in so often, and another time, the therapist told us we should allow Lucy to eat whenever and whatever she wanted. She even manipulated us, threatening not to eat if we didn't give her what she wanted.

The denial got to us, too. Lucy never admitted to a problem until she was forced into treatment because of a collapse or severe malnutrition. She would be sneaky about food and her weight, from one extreme to the other. During anorexia, she would lie and tell us she had eaten more than she had. With bulimia she denied eating food that we knew had been there the day before.

That simply wasn't the Lucy we had been used to. The Lucy before all this was kind and smart and funny. Everyone at school liked her and the phone rang constantly with calls from friends. The Lucy after is not very nice, and rarely laughs. All her friends have dropped her because they got bored of talking about food."

Impact on Family

For every parent I talked to, family life revolved around the eating disordered child, at least in the early stages of the illness. The impact of this was the number one stressor for many mothers and fathers. This included the havoc that affected the entire family, as well as problems that arose between husband and wife (where both were present and dealing with the child). One mother was shocked when her husband reacted in anger to their daughter:

"A lot of things were said. My husband got pretty loud at one point, while trying to get her to see she had to make some steps in the right direction. He told her if she didn't she wasn't going to be allowed to stay in the house. I was devastated."

The impact on marriages was profound. In one situation, both the mother and father felt so physically ill over the situation the father had to take time off work. In another, a mother shared that she feared her husband was so stressed he would drop over from a heart attack or stroke.

On an emotional level, responses between husbands and wives were varied. One mom was in charge of most of the day-to-day caregiving and would get angry with the dad when he didn't do things the way she wanted. In another situation a husband had a hard time talking about the eating disorder and refused to go to therapy, which left his wife to face the therapist alone. Another set of parents found themselves exhausted physically as well as mentally. They said as time went on they were more rather than less worried. Another couple said the joy was no longer in their lives since having to cope with their daughter's eating disorder; both exhaustion and worry had diminished it.

Sometimes the impact was long-term, as it was for this mom:

"I let her eating disorder distance me from family and friends. It controlled me and dictated how I should live my life. Now I am totally on my own and trying to deal with it, and, I might add, very lonely."

A mom who admits her marriage was already in trouble describes her daughter's eating disorder as the breaking point. She and her husband divorced just around the time her daughter switched from anorexia to compulsive overeating.

Career Impact

The impact of an eating disorder on parents' professional lives was more profound for mothers, who seemed to shoulder the day-to-day responsibility for care and to make it a priority over other activities. This is not to suggest fathers were uninvolved in care — their support came in other ways. They recognized the need for a continuous income and the associated health care benefits of full-time employment, so leaving their jobs simply was not an option.

In two cases, mothers quit work because balancing the needs of daughters with the demands of work became overwhelming, and there seemed to be no other choice. Both of these women felt lucky to have additional financial support from extended family, because their salaries were clearly missed at the same time additional expenses related to health care arose.

Some General Legal Observations on FMLA

Trips to doctors and therapists, lost weeks from work for family days at residential treatment centers, and the other hundred reasons why the parent of a child with an eating disorder has to miss work, can cause tremendous difficulties for that parent with his or her employer. Some employers make an effort to work with the parent in dealing with the myriad absences that accompany a child's eating disorder; others do not. Even the most reasonable of employers grows frustrated with the absences caused by the severely ill child with anorexia or bulimia. These frustrations, and the accompanying fear of a lost job, increase the stresses brought by the simple act of being parent to an eating disorder victim.

The law provides some help for parents in these circumstances. The *Family Medical Leave Act* ("FMLA") allows an employee to take up to twelve weeks off from work during a twelve month period to deal with their own serious health condition or the serious health condition of a parent or child. At the end of that twelve week period the FMLA requires the employer to reinstate the employee to the same or equivalent job with no loss in seniority. While the FMLA does not require paid leave, it does require the employer to pay the employee's health insurance premiums during that twelve week period exactly as if the employee were still working.

The twelve week period does not have to be taken in a single twelve week increment or even in increments of a week or a day. It can be taken as parts of a work day and therefore cover an employee who must take a child for a doctor or therapist's visit. It can be taken in longer periods for Family Weeks at treatment centers. [One mother reported she took worked half days for 24 consecutive weeks to deal not only with doctor visits and similar obligations but to spend more time with her child when she returned home from school or did not attend school in an effort to provide care and reassurance.]

An employer cannot deny its employee properly documented family leave chosen in increments convenient to the employee. To the extent practicable the FMLA requires the employee give advance notice of the need for leave, preferably thirty days, but FMLA recognizes that in many instances the need for leave is unforeseeable and no advance notice can be given.

FMLA is available only in businesses which employ at least fifty persons which does leave some parents working for small companies without the law's protection. An employer can require, and most do, that during FMLA leave the employee utilize any accrued sick leave and vacation time before going on unpaid leave. While FMLA does not alleviate the financial burden of lost wages for time devoted to caregiving its guarantee of continued health insurance and reinstatement to employment can be of enormous benefit to some families. Source*: Paul J. Dellasega, JD*

Other mothers couldn't leave work because they were either single parents or their families simply could not survive the loss of income. In these cases, the stress was often tremendous, especially if the woman chose not to tell her employer about her daughter's illness. A situation of needing to leave work to transport to doctor's appointments or attend to crises created tension for these women as they struggled to stay at their jobs.

One mother who was advised to take a leave from her job confessed that she'd refused, because she felt going to work was a welcome distraction from the crisis at home. She did, however, cut back on her hours. Another mother went back to work part time to help with expenses, but found work was actually helpful in keeping her mind off things.

Staying at work proved problematic for some moms. Juggling appointments and crises with job responsibilities nearly led one mother to lose her position as a school teacher:

"I was getting calls all the time because she was cutting or there was some other problem. It was uncomfortable. Everyone knew what was going on, from other teachers and the administration to all my daughter's friends.

I missed so much time in the spring, when kids were preparing for standardized testing, and parents were upset I wasn't there to work with their kids. Some even questioned why I was teaching if I couldn't control my family. Luckily, my boss previously had some experience with eating disorders in his family, so he was extremely understanding."

One mother did say the impact on her career was positive because she is a counselor and grew to understand eating disorders better.

Bulimia versus Anorexia

Although parents didn't describe a diagnosis of bulimia as more stressful than pure anorexia, this seemed to be the case. Although the mess of the house after a binge and purge episode was referred to openly, the diagnosis of bulimia was not. Often, a child who began with anorexia and restricting would "convert" to bulimia, which parents found more distressing because the behaviors were so constant and visible. (It is not unusual for a switch from anorexia to bulimia to occur.) Some authorities seem to agree that bulimia is more stigmatized, perhaps because a romantic notion of anorexia persists (see http://www.medicinenet.com/bulimia/article.htm).

"I don't think people realize what shame bulimics carry with them forever, even worse than anorexics because our disease is so 'ugly.'" [Posted on message board about eating disorders]

The stresses I heard about were many and intense, and some parents felt there would never be a challenge in their lives equivalent to caregiving for a son or daughter with anorexia or bulimia. Although many saw their situations as at least partially due to faulty parenting, in reality some of the most profound examples of love for a child I have ever heard came from these moms and dads, who persisted through so much with such little reward.

16
Support Systems
Big and Small

꙳⸙꙳

"WE DIDN'T TELL ANYONE. WE'RE VERY PRIVATE." MOTHER
OF A YOUNG ADULT GIRL WITH ANOREXIA

"WE SPENT A LOT OF TIME WITH ANOTHER FAMILY WHO
HAD GONE THROUGH THIS. IT REALLY HELPED. WE HAD
BEEN LOOKING FOR SOMEONE WHO KNEW HOW IT WAS."
FATHER OF A GIRL WITH ANOREXIA

Wendy had been a successful real estate agent before retiring to raise her two children. While they were growing up, she worked part-time at several small businesses: once as an interior decorator, and for a few years, as a caterer. Her husband Ben made a good living as an engineer, so there was no pressure for her to work unless she wanted to.

Wendy didn't want to. She loved being a mom, and knew that until her children left for college, she wanted to be at home and available for them. Her part-time jobs always took second place to school functions or any event involving her older son Chris, or her daughter Nadia.

When she and Ben discovered that Chris was struggling with bulimia, Wendy's world fell apart. She withdrew from all her friends, ashamed of what she'd learned, and berated herself for being a "bad mother." Many days while her children were at school she couldn't stop crying or sitting in one place, feeling depressed. As soon as Chris came home from school she would observe him closely, offering to go on walks or otherwise distract him so he wouldn't binge or purge. The harder she tried, the worse his bulimia became.

"It's almost like he's defying me when he does it," she told Ben. For his part, Ben "ordered" his son to stop throwing up and start eating normally. Chris received these commands silently, but his binging and purging continued.

Wendy tearfully asked Chris what she could do to make him better, but he told her the bulimia wasn't about her mothering skills. In spite of his dismissal, she repeatedly asked Louise, Chris's therapist, what she had done wrong, and if there was anything she could do differently to help her son. She telephoned Louise so often the therapist suggested Wendy might need professional counseling too.

In the next three months, Chris's bulimia did not worsen, nor did it improve. Weekly visits to Louise and regular visits to the medical doctor helped him stay stable, although he had occasional mood swings. Pressured by her son, Wendy kept his eating disorder a secret from everyone, including her parents, who questioned why Chris ate so much during their Christmas vacation visit, but never seemed to gain weight.

Nadia, on the other hand, continued to thrive, bringing home high grades and excelling in soccer. She seemed almost the perfect child, and rarely gave Wendy or Ben cause to worry.

It was Wendy who seemed to experience the most overt distress of anyone in her family. The day-to-day stress of seeing Chris harm his body made her depressed and angry. Sometimes she felt physically ill or had crippling headaches that kept her in bed for days. Finally, Ben urged her to find a therapist for herself, as he no longer knew how to deal with her ongoing grief.

When Louise suggested the same thing (again), Wendy, still convinced it was not going to help, reluctantly agreed. While Chris and Nadia were at school, she began to meet with Sonya, a social worker who had dealt with many mothers who had children in crisis. Patiently, she listened to Wendy's story during their first visit, then looked her squarely in the eyes.

"So you feel like a bad mom, a bad wife, and a bad person. Where does that leave you Wendy?"

The question opened up a vault of fear in Wendy as she admitted she was terrified of the future. During her subsequent visits, she and Sonya explored many issues surrounding Wendy's self concept: her feelings about her own mother, who had been a busy physician with little time for her children, her shyness during high school, and the difficulty she'd had making friends, and finally, the infertility problems that preceded her pregnancy with Chris.

Bit by bit, Wendy began to come to terms with what she perceived to be a failed mothering experience. Bolstered by an antidepressant Sonya's physician colleague prescribed, she developed a plan for dealing with both her feelings and the need to cope with Chris's behaviors on a day-to-day basis. Ben accompanied her for a few sessions, and began to understand how important it was for him to take a more active role with his son.

Although Wendy would far rather have a son who is bulimia-free, she admits that Chris's problems provided the impetus for her to work on some issues of her own. Most days, she doesn't blame herself for her son's eating disorder, and she's resumed her part-time work as an interior decorator.

Two weeks after restarting her job, she met Carolyn, a funny, bright woman she'd known and admired from the school PTO. When Carolyn mentioned that her daughter was bulimic, Wendy was nearly speechless. For the first time, she shared with another person her son's eating disorder. From that point on, Carolyn and she became each other's strongest support systems.

Parents of children with eating disorder often put their own needs at the bottom of a long list of "to-do's" as they desperately attempt to help their children. Like Wendy and the parents in the previous chapter, their list of stressors is long, and the support systems woefully inadequate.

The Strain of Secrets

One of the best sources of help — a parent like Carolyn — was simply unavailable for those parents who chose not to tell. For three years, one family kept their daughter's eating disorder secret. While the young woman's friends knew she was bulimic, her extended family did not. This added to the mother's sense of shame, which was compounded because her daughter was also a cutter. Now she wishes she had found a confidant, as her recent connections with other parents of children with anorexia and bulimia has helped tremendously.

Finding Your Voice

Telling the story of a child's eating disorder helps clarify a family's situation and can garner support for parents. Most of the mothers and fathers I spoke with commented on how helpful it was to share their experiences, and even thanked me for giving them the opportunity to do so!

The perception of helping others clearly benefited parents who shared their stories. Many moms used the energy generated by upsetting emotions to become eating disorder activists, or made an effort to reach out to others.

Those Who Help and Those Who Don't

Yet the wrong kind of friends can cause more problems than they help with. A mom found it difficult to deal with suspicious friends who commented on her daughter's "high metabolism." It was her perception they were fishing for details about her daughter's bulimia, rather than truly concerned. Another mom echoed this sentiment by saying she had one friend who insisted on knowing the child's weight each time they met.

"You need to talk to those who have been there," it was affirmed, again and again. "Only someone who has gone through this can truly understand." How does one find these "others?" While support groups are available in some communities, they received mixed reviews.

"Not helpful at all," was one comment, while another said, "It saved my life." Much of the benefit of support groups seemed derived from the structure imposed by its leader. Where there was concrete information given, the sessions seemed more helpful.

Word of mouth appears to be a far better way of finding another parent with similar family situations. In smaller towns, parents would approach others they knew who had a child with an eating disorder. Sometimes the parents were approached by experienced others who heard about their situation and voluntarily made contact. One woman said she had deliberately told the physician who treated her daughter to feel free to use her as a referral source for other parents.

"I'm starting my own informal network, where parents can find someone who has gone through the process," another mother shared. "This way when a newbie needs information or just has a question, they can call and talk to a mom or dad who understands."

It's a Family Affair

During times of self doubt, one father said family input was helpful to reassure the correctness of decisions. He had a large group of brothers and sisters, one of whom had experienced a child with eating disorders. They were always helpful in talking things over, afterwards, he felt glad his conclusion was based on the sound judgment of many people not in the midst of a like crisis, but who cared about his daughter.

When asked to speak about things that could be done to help parents, the replies were plentiful. In addition to points already made in other chapters, these "do's and don'ts" were suggested as things that they will tell a caregiving mother or father.

The Do's and Don'ts from Caregiving Parents

Things that are helpful:

Let go and let God. Faith, prayer, and a religious community are a strong source of support. Sometimes, prayer is the most tangible thing that can be done for a child, and you'll feel as if others are sharing your burden.

Substitute physical activity for angry responses to child. Go for a walk instead of screaming back during angry outbursts.

Be assured that your child isn't the only one, or the sickest. It's surprising to learn how many other parents in your immediate environment have gone through similar experiences. Don't assume you are alone in your situation just because other families seem well adjusted.

Maintain hope. Most children with eating disorders improve. Listen to the stories of those whose children are in recovery.

Draw a line for self preservation. Once you have done everything you can, recognize that a child has to be motivated to change his or her behavior before it will happen. You can't do it for the child (or you probably would have by now).

Get treatment for all aspects of the disorder, medical, psychological, and spiritual.

Take care of yourself. Attend to your own health and take time to give yourself some extras occasionally: a day away or anything that will help you have a breather.

See a therapist if you need one, and don't feel bad about taking antidepressant medication if that's suggested. These are depressing situations!

Focus on behavior, not weight. Your day to day life is influenced more by the child's behavior, which goes hand in hand with weight.

Stay on the same page as your spouse and present a united front. Both parents should plan out consequences for behaviors and other issues that need to be addressed related to the eating disorder.

Journal. Write about your stress, or keep a record of events. It will help you see the big picture rather than one bad day.

Look at the lessons you've learned. Feel good about the caregiving skills you have developed, and your persistence in caring for your child.

Use online support groups. If you find support groups beneficial, there are several support groups for families only which can be accessed through the Internet. They will connect you with a much larger community of caregiving parents who have similar experiences as you.

List the child's good qualities. Don't lose sight of the child he or she was, and will be again in the future. See and comment on the positives that are still there despite the eating disorder.

Set long and short term goals. Be realistic about what to expect. One less binge is better than no change at all.

Learn as much as you can about eating disorders. Go to websites intended for researchers or health care professionals as they offer the best information. Find a friend who is a doctor or nurse to help "interpret" if needed.

Stay consistent with doctor and therapist visits. Not only will this make scheduling easier, it will help you orient your care around visits.

Contact schools and coaches for input on their perceptions of how your child is doing. You don't need to tell your child you are doing this, but it may be reassuring. Many children function better with peers than parents.

Help promote public awareness about eating disorders. Share your experience if you feel comfortable and your child doesn't mind.

Get competent professionals involved to share responsibility.

Use doctors and therapists who will reliably return phone calls and be available during emergencies, and talk to them about how they can help with specific aspects of care. Some examples would be:

Therapists who agree to develop a contract with the child for eating behaviors and to hold the child accountable. This frees you from having to negotiate around food and eating.

Doctors who will weigh the child regularly and inform him or her of the consequences that will occur if extreme loss occurs. In this way, you don't have to keep track of weight or argue with a child about changing behaviors he or she believes will cause weight gain.

Doctors who will let child know when she or he is in the "danger zone" and will take action to intervene. For example, one doctor restricted a girl's activity and talked to her about the possibility of an eating-disorder-induced heart attack. Although parents can say the same thing, it means more when it comes from an expert or authority.

Things not to do:
Use a "tough love" approach: It doesn't work with eating disorders.

Forget the needs of your other children. Find people to help with transportation, etc. and give some extra attention to siblings on a regular basis.

Neglect your spouse. Make a point of going out to dinner from time to time without your children and put talk about eating disorders off limits!

Blame yourself — you're NOT the cause. Over time, you will recognize there are so many different families out there where children have anorexia or bulimia they couldn't have all made the same mistake.

Ignore the problem because you don't want it to be true. In the long run, it will make things worse.

Think the child can be "cured" by someone or something else — if there was a magic treatment, eating disorders would be nonexistent.

Avoid hospitalization if it's indicated: It might be the intervention your child needs.

Continue to use professionals who make you feel bad. You are paying them, so if you have a choice, go elsewhere. If you don't have a choice, arrange to speak to the individual privately about your perceptions and feelings.

How Friends and Family Can Help

In addition to suggestions about things a mother or father could do internally, here are some of the ways parents felt others can be supportive:

Don't be afraid to ask about how the child is doing. Genuine concern is appreciated, but don't press if the parent seems to prefer not to discuss it.

Don't tell someone you "know how they feel" or understand how difficult it is to be a caregiver for a child with an eating disorder: you don't. A better way would be to tell the person you're sorry they're going through difficult times, or, better yet, ask if there's anything you can do to help, at the time of contact and later.

Don't comment on how thin a child is and ask what the parents are doing about it.

Don't make comments about weight gain to the child or tell him or her "You look healthy." This is often interpreted as "You look fat."

Don't push food, try to convince the child to eat, or get engaged in long conversations about food with the child.

Don't bring up the child's eating disorder in front of others. If the parents want to talk about it, they will.

Do offer to help out with transportation or other caregiving activities. Offer to do something with the child so parents get some time off.

Do inform yourself about eating disorders, but don't think that you are an authority.

If appropriate and desired, connect parents with others you know who have children with eating disorders.

Do listen without giving advice. The worst comments are things like: "Just make him eat," or "My kid likes food too much to get an eating disorder," or "I wouldn't let my child get away with things like that."

Do send a card or email to the parent, letting them know you are thinking about them.

Although it may feel like additional "work" to create a network of resources for yourself, these parents suggest it's well worth taking the time to do it. It's one investment you'll make that's guaranteed to bring a sound return.

RESOURCES

http://web1.iop.kcl.ac.uk/iop/Departments/PsychMed/EDU/
CarerEmotions.shtml
Discussion of family responses to caregiving for children with ED.

http://web1.iop.kcl.ac.uk/iop/Departments/PsychMed/EDU/
Carerexperiences.shtml
Accounts from parents who were caregivers.

http://www.angelfire.com/mi/anorexia/parents.html
The story of "Mike" a dad whose daughter is (was) anorexic.

17
The Light At the End of the Tunnel: Recovery

കൃക്

"All I can say is it was a miracle."

"I can't explain why it happened, or how it stopped, but I say a lot of prayers of thanks now that it's over."

"He finally realized how much this illness was damaging him."

From parents whose children have recovered

Charlie's seventeen-year-old daughter Erin was four years into her eating disorder when he began to question whether she would ever recover. Although he hadn't talked with other fathers about what happened when he left work each day, he dreaded heading home, wondering as he drove the short distance if Erin was having a good day. If the day had gone badly, he would sometimes receive frantic calls from his wife Connie, who seemed to be a lightening rod for Erin's emotions.

"I know she's in there throwing up," Connie would sob into the phone. "There's nothing I can do to stop her! She came home from school and called me a 'bitch' the minute she walked in the door. Then she headed for the kitchen, and from there right to the bathroom. I can't watch her destroy herself anymore."

The entire family had learned in the first year that Erin's status was a weathervane for everyone else; if she did well they did too, and vice versa. All too often, she was doing badly.

In year two, Charlie accidentally discovered that Rick, the father of Erin's best friend, had gone through much of the worry, anxiety, and tension he was experiencing. Rick's daughter had suffered from anorexia for two brief but intense years that were marked by frequent hospitalizations and visits to the Emergency Room.

"Somehow, after two years of it, she got better," Rick told Charlie. He had no explanation for what made his daughter recover beyond "prayer."

As a consequence of his conversations with Rick, Charlie expected that Erin, too, would recover at the two year mark, or shortly thereafter. When she didn't, he began to wonder if her doctors really knew what they were doing, and if there might not be a better program for his daughter.

By year three, he was desperate, begging Erin to eat normally and constantly feeling as if it was his role to run interference between his daughter and Connie. Erin's bulimia began to involve long stretches of anorexia, which challenged him further. Which was worse: a daughter who wouldn't eat anything, or a daughter who ate constantly and threw up every bite?

Erin ended up in an eating disorder treatment facility for two months during year four. By the time of admission, she was as sick as Charlie had ever seen her, and he worried she might not survive. Several times, he met Rick for lunch and confided his fears, which was surprisingly helpful since Rick, too, had seen his daughter close to death.

Charlie and Connie visited Erin weekly in the treatment center, but it wasn't until they attended a mandatory "Family Week" that they noticed things changing. During that week, Charlie, Connie, and their grown son Justin spent five days at the facility, learning about eating disorders and attending intensive therapy sessions with Erin. In one of those meetings, Charlie learned that although Justin was away at college, he had worried constantly about her sister's health, and had seen one of the counselors in the student health center because he was so anxious he couldn't concentrate on classes.

When Erin came home from the treatment center, she voluntarily spent her summer in a partial hospitalization program for eating disorders near their house. Gradually she progressed to attending a support group, and seeing her therapist and family doctor weekly. She clearly continued to vomit, but the frequency had diminished, and she rarely binged.

Two months after her discharge from inpatient care, Erin told Charlie she was beginning to think she might be able to get better. He wondered if these feelings were related to Todd, a neighborhood boy she was spending time with. Todd seemed to bring out the best in Erin, making her laugh and relax like the girl she had been before her eating disorder.

"It wasn't the same as it was for Rick," Charlie recalls. "This was bit by bit. Connie called it 'baby steps' and I think that's exactly what it was, a trying things out, let's see how this might feel kind of thing."

When we spoke, it had been six years since Charlie first learned about his daughter's eating disorder. Although Connie told him Erin still binges and purges when she's under stress or something traumatic happens, he feels she is, for the most part, recovered.

"I can live with it once every so often. Every day, even every week would bother me, but it's so much better than it was I'm grateful. And I think it will gradually taper off and disappear completely. I didn't get a miracle like Rick did, but hey, I'll take it. I'm not worried she'll drop over with a heart attack because she's so malnourished — I haven't worried about that in what seems like a long time."

Most of the children of parents I interviewed have improved in some way. Their healing was most often a process that took place over months and even years, with "recovery" being redefined again and again. In some cases, getting better meant total abstinence from eating disordered behavior while for others, less frequent eating disordered behavior and better overall health was acceptable.

Reality Check

As the journey through anorexia and bulimia progressed, parents came to understand that relapses did not mean a total slide back into the acute phase, or, if they did, the process back to recovery was often shorter or less intense. Most often, cycles of hope and frustration and progress and setbacks gradually led to recovery.

"This is a process, a battle where we have to take one day at a time and be thankful they are still in our lives so we at least have an opportunity to try and influence them," said one mother whose daughter had recently been discharged from an eating disorder center. She observed that her child was much improved, but still had difficulty with some eating behaviors.

"It's like she's been through hell, and now she's back," said another, whose child appears completely free of eating disordered behaviors.

A third mom offers: "She is making steady, little gains. I compare how she is now to how she was last year at this time, and I'm so grateful."

"Seven years after recovery, my daughter still goes to therapy and notices her eating disordered behaviors flare up when her mood is low. She still is struggling with it, but it hasn't been a major preoccupation for a year," was yet another observation.

Unlike the expectations they might have had during the initial phase, parents no longer believed that doctors and therapists were able to make the child's eating disorder better and understood that the child's motivation was — and had been all along — the crucial first step.

Ever After

The profile of a family with a child in recovery varied greatly. Sometimes, life proceeded on for the son or daughter as if the eating disorder had never occurred, and memories of it were consciously avoided. In other situations, therapies such as medications or counseling were continued in an effort to maintain the progress made.

Even when the active stage of the eating disorder ended, the impact of ongoing stress was felt, much as other people who experience a major life trauma report. Both parents and siblings had long-term anxieties over the recovery of their loved one, often voicing a concern that relapse would occur. Years later, it was not unusual for parents to hesitate before labeling their child "recovered" because they recognized that eating behaviors had become a way of coping for their son or daughter. In one case, a mom shared that: "Her boyfriend, who had been so steadfast and caring of her throughout her illness, broke up with her shortly after she seemed to be in recovery. It was like he had that problem, PTSD, and he just couldn't take it any more."

Another says: "I had post traumatic stress disorder, and so did my husband. Every time we talked about her, we cried. Every time she had a setback, we cried."

"Even though she has been in recovery for quite awhile, I think my parenting of her has been impacted permanently. I still respond to her needs and concerns with an underlying fear of the disease, or shall I say, a fear of its return to the active virulent form?"

A Fragile Acceptance

Parents worried that life changes and transition time might trigger a relapse. In particular, leaving home to go to college caused anxiety for mothers and fathers whose children were graduating from high school. One mother said: "Two years later, I still think every day about how fragile her recovery is. Every transition time is a worry to us. I look forward to the day when our lives can be in more of a balance with each of us getting our needs met. Both my husband and I feel as if our mental and physical health have been compromised."

Another mother confessed that she still responds to her daughter in a less than genuine way due to fear of relapse. She wishes she could return to the pre-eating disorder days when the communication between her and her daughter was more open as she felt they were very close, but that seems impossible.

"If she or he gets sick again, it will be almost too much," was a sentiment many voiced after describing a long course of illness. Seeing a child who had once been in the throes of a seemingly incurable illness was more bearable in some ways than seeing him or her recover then succumb to anorexia or bulimia again.

What, When, How, and Why

When asked about what prompts recovery, there were many thoughts but no certainties. All agreed that recovery was under the control of the child, and just as eating disorders are a disease about control, so is recovery.

Some other thoughts on recovery influences were:

"Little by little, I think with people not giving up and that is what we keep driving into her, that nobody is giving up on you, even if you want us to, we're not giving up."

"She got sick of having to live the way she did."

"A combination of maturity and family therapy. There was information and an emotional release from therapy which was astounding. Those things should really start up front as it would save a lot of time. Maturity plays a role as well — I don't know if our daughter could have done all this in just a year or two."

"We told our daughter (and, in one case a son) that we would not continue paying for college if she/he didn't seek treatment and at least try to recover."

"Her activities were limited every time she refused to eat. She hated the thought of missing school or having to stand on the sidelines during gym because her weight was too low."

"She got scared. There were effects on her heart, and the doctors told her she could die. That made her stop."

"When my daughter was hospitalized her doctor came in and confronted her point blank about her behavior and the harm it was doing to both her and those around her. Although she was furious over his comments, it made her think, and shortly thereafter she began to eat normally again. He helped more than a therapist who kept us in the dark for months."

"My daughter told me when she was in the hospital and would wake to see me sleeping in a chair at the side of her bed she realized how much I loved her, and that made her want to recover."

"The only thing I can say is prayer because I never thought it would happen. It's a miracle to me that it did."

Better than Before

Although it was hard to imagine there could ever be an end to the crisis of a serious eating disorder, this did in fact happen, and some couples and families found their connections not only renewed, but strengthened. On an individual basis, the need to deal with the serious health problem of a beloved child was sometimes the impetus for personal change. Some comments:

"My daughter's eating disorder forced me to face my fears as an example to her. That was helpful."

"In some ways her illness was a good thing. It helped us get therapy for our own issues."

"Her eating disorder and what we had to go through to support her has improved my marriage."

"In a weird sort of way, his bulimia did help my husband and I realize how very strong we were, both as individuals and as a pair. We'd had some tragedies before, and now dealing with this has really made us appreciate each other."

Amazingly, much good came from terrible experiences. In addition to improved individual and family functioning, outreach to others was a direct consequence of the caregiving experience. One mom started a support group in her small community so other parents could have what she searched for during her daughter's illness. Other mothers engaged in activities designed to prevent eating disorders for young girls and boys, or to raise awareness.

The following narrative tells such a story. Maryellen Clausen, founder of Ophelia's Place in Liverpool, New York, has lived for many years with two daughters who suffer from eating disorders, but has turned trauma into triumph. Here's what she shared:

Dear Cheryl:

"It's hard for me to remember my life before ED. It has been a journey filled with pain, frustration, exhaustion, devastation, however as a result I have discovered faith, peace, joy and hope. It was through the depletion of my resources that I discovered God's amazing grace.

I married my husband in 1990. He is my third husband — it took me three times to get it right! My first marriage ended when my daughter Nicole was only two. I suffered a breakdown and as a result her father was awarded custody. Shortly after

I married my second husband, Danny, I had my younger daughter Holli. When she was five he walked out and she never heard from him again.

My oldest daughter, Nicole was diagnosed in 1997 with an eating disorder. In addition to the family history I've shared, she had also survived a college date rape. Within two years she was in rough shape, using drugs and alcohol as well as cutting and abusing laxatives. During this time, Nicole disclosed to me that she had been abused by her father. I didn't have a clue.

It was horrible to see my oldest daughter in such deep pain and using whatever she could to numb it. I was overwhelmed and incredibly confused. Finally, she met the criteria for inpatient treatment, which lasted all of two weeks! After that, she returned to my house, and never went back to her dad's.

Her "recovery" lasted a month, tops. She ran away and became even more acute in her eating disorder, ending up back in the hospital after she slashed her wrists in a suicide attempt. This time she spent three months in treatment, and returned home to relapse again.

Over the next few years she cycled through a number of treatment programs, and survived major suicide attempts, each one more horrific than the previous. In the midst of all of this, Holli, our younger daughter, was diagnosed with an eating disorder. The truth is her anorexia began at a very young age, but was never discovered until she was sixteen.

Nicole's worst was the beginning of Holli's worst. Two daughters in crisis — it was hard to believe. At times, there seemed to be a competition between the girls. One would get angry at the other for doing the exact same thing she was doing. They both blamed each other for what the family was going through, and yet they were both acting in very similar ways.

How did this all come to be? What I was feeling through all of this? I'm not sure. It seemed incomprehensible to me to even try and understand. I rarely thought of how I felt because that was way too painful. Instead, I chose to focus on my daughters and their recovery, thinking I would deal with mine after I "fixed" them.

That was my focus and my goal. Through this all, I never wanted the girls to know how all of this impacted me, because it was my "job" to take care of them, and I was determined to do just that. I spent hours a day on the Internet researching "cures," I was always at the book store buying more books, and I made dozens of phone calls daily. I was driven to find "the answers!!!!" Oh, if only it was that simple.

By the summer of 2001, shortly after Holli's seventeenth birthday, she was admitted to an acute care program in Arizona for 4 ½ months. She returned home in December, determined to graduate from high school and put her eating disorder behind her. She did graduate, but less than a year later relapsed and went back to Arizona as an inpatient for three months. Family Week there was certainly a challenge for us, as you can imagine.

Holli has since embraced recovery, moved to Arizona, and become a Christian. For the summer of 2004 she is at home, volunteering at Ophelia's Place and sharing her message of hope and recovery.

Nicole is working aggressively on making healthier choices. As a result of her ED, she struggles with fibromyalgia, and irritable bowel syndrome, but for the first time I see a real desire in her to get better. For a very long time I never believed that she would survive this. As a matter of fact I heard a family share a message about the death of their daughter, and it greatly impacted on me. More than ever, I was convinced that the only way to deal with an ED is in a "no nonsense," in-your-face, zero tolerance way. We don't stand back and watch our children drown, or put their hand in fire, so why do we walk on egg shells with an ED? How have eating disorders gotten so much power?

Eating disorders impacted both my daughters' education. Nicole had dreams of becoming a doctor which are at least temporarily derailed. Holli has no desire to go back to college as school was a real trigger for her. She had made a decision at a very young age (seven or eight) that she couldn't be the smartest, most athletic, the prettiest, but she could be the smallest. She was throwing away her school lunch, and suffered from chronic headaches, stomach aches, she even passed out once in elementary school. Never did we suspect an eating disorder.

Our daughters' illnesses stressed our marriage financially, emotionally, and physically, but my husband was my best friend through every minute of this. Even when he didn't "get it," he was ALWAYS there for me, thank God.

As for me — I was no longer a mom, a wife, an executive, sister, daughter, or individual. I was the mom with two eating disordered daughters. It seemed to be what defined me, what defined all of us. Friendships ended, family members were frustrated, and even then there was so much I didn't share with anyone, fearing one of two things would happen: they would try to "fix" it or they would tell me they understood ... which they didn't. No one can comprehend this disease and the total impact it has on a family.

Nicole once told me this was her disease, but I told her it was all of ours. What we once knew was no longer, including the simple things like family dinner on Sundays.

How did Ophelia's Place come to be? Shortly after Holli returned from Arizona after her first admission there she commented on how she wished there was a place she could go to for support. I was inspired to look at that. After holding an open house and determining that it was the need of the community not just our own family's personal need Ophelia's Place started to take shape.

Through all of this Cheryl, I truly feel blessed. All of this has been used as a foundation on which Ophelia's Place has been built. It has been a true privilege and an honor for me to be a part of this. We have reached thousands of people with our message of awareness, we have created a wings of hope outreach, a book written by the "caterpillars" (a wee division of Ophelia's Place), consumer driven support groups offered three times a week, a family and friend support group, a major awareness campaign, and have commercials being played on the radio throughout central New York. In February 2005, we are sponsoring a two day state conference. I have had the incredible opportunity to be a venue for the voices of hope and recovery.

So I no longer wish to avoid the past but embrace it. I believe this is God's purpose for my life. I'm no longer just surviving, I am living.

Peace, Mary Ellen

July 2004

୬∘ஞ

Postscript

Among the medical students and residents, I am known as the," Adolescent Doctor." When they say this, it is not clear to me whether they mean that I am the physician at the medical center who takes care of teenagers or whether they actually think I act like an adolescent. In any event, I am the Director of Adolescent Medicine and the Director of the Eating Disorders Program at the Penn State Children's Hospital, Milton S. Hershey Medical Center. In that capacity, I have had the privilege of taking care of teens and young adults with eating disorders and their families for almost 10 years.

In that time, I have seen a lot of suffering. I have seen young girls literally on the exam room floor, too weak to sit or stand. I have seen girls who haven't eaten in two weeks, crying for food, but unable to eat because they want to become so thin that they can "disappear." I have seen older teens vomit after they eat, so much and so often that they bleed from their esophagus and vomit blood ... and then they vomit again.

I have seen adult women who have been struggling with their eating disorders all of their lives. That feel they have literally become their eating disorder; that it defines them as a person and they would cease to exist if they gave it up.

I have also seen the effect of these eating disorders on the families of the patients that I care for. I have seen families ripped apart by the stress imposed by caring for their children with anorexia nervosa. I have seen families seemly cursed with a cycle of abuse begun generations before. I have seen families in crisis, in divorce, and in turmoil.

But I have also seen amazing strength, amazing courage, and amazing grace in the face of despair. I have seen amazing recoveries. I have seen young women suffering from the stereotypes imposed by our media-driven culture conquer their fear of gaining weight, conquer their fear of eating, and with the help of their parents recover. I have witnessed a young woman suffering from abuse rise above her pain, recover from her eating disorder, get married, and have a baby. I have seen families pull together, strengthened by their shared experiences, and grow more in their love than they ever thought possible.

In my experience, the common thread in recovery is compassion. Compassion from the patients for themselves and for their families. Compassion from the family for their child and for themselves. And finally, compassion from us: those privileged to try and help them.

Our role is to offer the patients and families the tools to their recovery; to point the way to the "Gateless Gate" which is always there, even if it seems unreachable. Medicines are a tool; therapy is a tool; groups are a tool. All of our programs, including outpatient treatment, evening and day treatment, and even inpatient treatment are tools. The purpose of our entire team, which includes medical specialists, psychiatrists, dieticians and therapists, is to help motivate the patient and then point the way to recovery.

The family is often the key. Only family members can offer the unconditional love and acceptance that can facilitate a young person's recovery. Only family can provide the strength, the backbone, from which a child can derive the will to take those first difficult steps down the formidable path to recovery. For it truly is a path, a road, and a journey.

Eating disorders do not occur overnight or in a vacuum. They also do not get better overnight or in a vacuum. They get better from the young person's commitment, patience, and persistence, even in the face of adversity. And they get better with the family right there, helping, encouraging, sometimes pushing, and always loving.

The message therefore is always hopeful. Recovery is always possible through love, compassion and acceptance.

Richard L. Levine, M.D., 2004
Professor of Pediatrics
Penn State College of Medicine
Director of Adolescent Medicine
Director, Eating Disorders Program
Penn State Children's Hospital
Milton S. Hershey Medical Center

Appendix A
In an Ideal World

The following thoughts were gleaned from parents who had a son or daughter with anorexia or bulimia. During a speaking engagement, I asked them what they would like from the professionals who treat their children.

Help us understand that denial [by the child] is the first stage of eating disorders so we don't take it personally.

Educate parents about eating disorders. Tell them that children with bulimia may binge and purge many times a day (as appropriate).

Help parents realize they cannot "talk" others out of their denial or behavior.

Stress that there is no rational answer to an irrational problem.

Avoid giving advice unless asked for (institutions, books).

Prepare parents for mood swings and anger, and help them realize they are part of starvation behavior. Develop a SPECIFIC plan to deal with anger, which will be different with each child.

Encourage parents to be mindful of other children in the house.

Suggest other adults help provide support when the parent is away.

Provide resources for financial assistance.

Be consistent in communication. One team member shouldn't withhold information "due to confidentiality" while others disclose it.

Reassure parents about their love and care for their children. Focus on what they HAVE done, rather than what they HAVEN'T.

Listen carefully to what parents say and address the "hidden message."

Be honest — tell parents their child's status. It's helpful for parents to have an idea of where their child is in the disorder.

Be available by phone.

Share the treatment plan for acute care with them so the "fear of death" can be addressed.

Offer to meet separately with parents to address their needs related to their child's eating disorder.

Get the whole story before taking action.

Find something to compliment them on about their child.

Stress that <u>both</u> parents should be involved in therapy.

Teach parents what and what not to monitor.

Take responsibility for monitoring a child's weight.

Give tips on how to deal with food behaviors (binging, purging, restricting, *etc.*).

Prepare parents for feeling guilt and shame, and stress that these are normal reactions.

Allow parents to help in planning and obtaining care.

Discourage child from venting anger at parents in inappropriate ways.

Encourage parents to journal and record their experiences. Have them highlight problems they want to talk to you about when they have a visit.

Connect parents with other parents who are further along in the process and have them discuss concern.

In contrast to what parents had to say, the next set of comments were made by a diverse group of healthcare professionals who were asked what they thought caregiving families of children with eating disorders needed to know. Here is what they would tell a parent:

Don't become a "hawk mother;" allow your daughter to have autonomy in her life.

Let your child know you will love him or her whether or not he or she gets better.

Eating disorders are a symptom of underlying issue— depression, anxiety, low self esteem, etc.

Pay attention to the child.

Have patience and consistency.

Take time to ask what you can do to help and listen.

Talk to your child.

The single piece of advice would be to <u>don't give up</u>!

Be patient.

Be there for your child.

Do not make mealtime a battle.

Let your child know that fear is okay and you would like to help carry it.

You cannot force your child to speak, but you can always be there to listen to verbal and non-verbal communication.

Be patient and love your child as you always have.

Affirm their value.

Remain open, receptive, and empathic to your child and his/her issues/lives.

There are many reasons for an eating disorder — try not to blame yourself.

Do not judge.

Do not blame yourself. Contribute to your child's recovery.

Listen.

Persevere while loving unconditionally.

Listen to your child and start/continue to express love, affirmation of your child's whole self.

Remember to take care of yourself . . . seek therapy or support for yourself.

Support and listen to your child. Be involved in your child's life.

Communicate concern not condemnation/criticism.

Don't keep any "bad" foods in the house — gallon of ice cream, bag of cookies, chips. The urge to binge won't be as strong if these foods aren't readily available in the house.

Don't become the "food police" (don't get into a power struggle).

I would say, "Tell your child that he/she is loved and is a good, special person."

You didn't cause this.

Be willing to be honest about how your family functions or doesn't.

Don't focus on the weight and food, get help.

Always let your child know you love her for who she is—that who she is includes much more than weight.

You and your child are each "enough" as you are.

It is not your "fault" or your child's, so try to get help for you and your child as you try to negotiate the difficult process of maintaining communication and patience while coping with fear and worry.

Listen and be supportive.

Support the therapy.

Focus on the child's state of mind and feelings. Set behavioral boundaries but do not take control away.

Don't expect this to be solved overnight.

Offer empathic communication to your child. <u>Listen</u> in a nonjudgmental way.

Get help from multidisciplinary team of professionals that work with educating patients.

Do not push perfection — make sure that you are not adding to the problem by your actions and or words.

Get your child specialized professional help.

Be available.

If you're struggling with depression, seek help. Let go of control with the child.

Continue to be supportive and not critical, encouraging communication.

Don't disparage your own body in front of your child. Example: "my butt is so big," "do my thighs look fat?"

Sit back, stop blaming and listen.

Family therapy when appropriate.

Both sets of comments were collected anonymously from parents and healthcare professionals during many speaking engagements throughout 2001-2004.

Appendix B
Websites

In addition to those listed throughout the book, here are some other helpful websites:

http://www.boston.com/yourlife/health/fitness/articles/2003/12/30/the_ancestry_of_anorexia/
Article by Shan Guisinger on families and eating disorders.

http://web1.iop.kcl.ac.uk/iop/Departments/PsychMed/EDU/GettingStarted.shtml
Excellent interview with a therapist at the Maudsley Institute and a family member.

http://www.nice.org.uk/pdf/cg009publicinfoenglish.pdf
Downloadable 2004 booklet on eating disorders from Britain's National Health Service.

http://www.aacap.org/publications/factsfam/eating.htm
Very good fact sheet from the American Academy of Child and Adolescent Psychiatry.

http://www.pale-reflections.com/getting_help.asp?page=what
Types of treatment for EDs.

http://www.anad.org/site/anadweb/section.php?id=2106
ANAD site has hotlines, referral services, support groups.

http://www.anad.org/site/anadweb/section.php?id=6605
ANAD site has a page on "Finding the Right Therapist" and "Inpatient/Outpatient Programs."

http://www.nationaleatingdisorders.org/
p.asp?WebPage_ID=286&Profile_ID=41153
NEDA site, page named "Navigating the System: Tips for Getting Treatment" advice on treatment and insurance issues, criteria for different levels of care, plus links for more info.

http://www.something-fishy.org/treatmentfinder.php
Something Fishy has a "Treatment finder" with listings of therapists and treatment facilities by state and area code.

http://www.edreferral.com/movement_therapy_&ed.htm
ED Referral had a page dedicated to Dance and Movement therapy.

http://www.edreferral.com/Referral%20Request.htm
ED Referral's referral system/database. This website claims to have been featured on Nova, the PBS science show. States it is the most comprehensive and easiest to search.

http://inside.bard.edu/academic/specialproj/darling/
adprob.htm
An informative website on adolescent health problems with a thorough discussion of anorexia and bulimia.

http://www.anad.org/site/anadweb/
content.php?type=1&id=6901
This web page has a through list of types of therapy and therapeutic terms with good definitions.

http://www.edreferral.com/treatment.htm
ED Referral explains levels of inpatient care very well.

http://www.nationaleatingdisorders.org/
p.asp?WebPage_ID=295&Profile_ID=41150
NEDA provides another good overview of treatment for eating
disorders. It reminds readers that individual treatment will vary
and provides links to other related pages on site.

http://www.nationaleatingdisorders.org/
p.asp?WebPage_ID=295&Profile_ID=41150
NEDA compiled five pages of topics each with a brief summary
and link to a longer explanation. Topics range from defining
the different types of eating disorders to advice for patients,
family, and professionals.

http://www.gurze.com/indexNEDA.htm
NEDA link with books and newsletters about eating disorders.

http://www.something-fishy.org/other/organizations.php
Something Fishy has this section dedicated to the names,
addresses, and phone numbers (as well as web links) to eating
disorder organizations and advocacy groups.

http://www.something-fishy.org/other/websites.php
Something Fishy has this section which organized web links
into categories like: online support sites, ED organizations,
Treatment Finder, Info & Support sites, personal sites,
promotional or special feature sites, *etc.*

Bibliography

Andersen, R.E., *et al.* (1995). Weight loss, psychological and nutritional patterns in competitive male body builders. *International Journal of Eating Disorders*, 18, 49-57.

Andersen, ROE. (1995). Eating disorders in males. In K. Brownell, K. & Fairburn, C.G., (Eds.), *Eating Disorders and Obesity: A Comprehensive Handbook*. New York: Guilford Publications, Inc.

Anderson, N. and Quarles, M. (2003). *Overcoming Addictive Behavior*. Ventura, CA: Regal Press.

Austrian, S. (2000). *Mental Disorders, Medications, and Clinical Social Work*. NY: Columbia University Press.

Becker, A. (1999), "Current concepts: Eating disorders." *New England Journal of Medicine*. Volume 340 (14), 1092-1098.

Christian, S. (1996). "Working with groups to explore food and body connection." Deluth, MN: Whole Person Associates, Inc.

Collins, L. (2005). *Eating with your anorexic: How my child recovered through family based treatment and yours can too*. New York, McGraw Hill.

Department of Health and Human Services (1987, 1995). *Anorexia Nervosa and Bulimia*. Washington DC: DHHS

DM, Garfinkel PE (Eds.). (1997). *Handbook of Treatment for Eating Disorders*, (2nd ed.). New York: The Gilford Press.

Fairburn, CG, Brownell, KD (Eds.) (2002). *Eating Disorders and Obesity*, 2nd edition. New York, Guilford.

Goff, K. (1998). Getting a grip on getting fit. *The Washington Times*, March 3.

Gorrell, C. (2001). Finding fault: Magazines may be abetting-though not aiding-An epidemic of eating disorders. *Psychology Today*, Volume 34.

Johnston, A. (1996). *Eating by the Light of the Moon.* Oceanside, CA: Gurze Press.

Kearney-Cooke, A., & Steichen-Asch, P. (1990). Men, body image, and eating disorders. In A. Andersen (Ed.), "Males with eating disorders," p. 47, New York: Brunner/Mazel.

Kirkpatrick, J., & Caldwell, P. (2005). *Eating Disorders: Everything you need to know* (YOUR PERSONAL HEALTH) Firefly Books Ltd; Revised edition.

Kolodny, N. (2004). *The Beginner's Guide to Eating Disorders Recovery.* Oceanside, CA: Gurze Books.

Latimer, J. (2000). *Beyond the Food Game.* Portland, OR: LivingQuest Publishing.

Levine, M. (1995). "Fear of fat." NEA Today, Vol. 14.

Lock J, Le Grange D, Agras S, *et al.* (2001). *Treatment Manual for Anorexia Nervosa: A family-based approach.* New York: The Guilford Press.

Maine, M. (1991). *Father Hunger: Fathers, Daughters and Food* Oceanside, CA: Gurze Books

Manton, C. (1999). *Fed up: Women and food in America.* New York: Bergin & Garvey.

Maurer, D., & Sobal, J. (1995). *Eating Agendas: Food and Nutrition as Social Problems*. Aldine de Gruyter.

Merrell, K. (1999). "Behavioral, Social, and Emotional Assessment of Children and Adolescents." Lawrence Erlbaum Associates.

Mehler, P. & Andersen, A. (1999). *Eating Disorders: A Guide to Medical Care and Complications,* 1st edition. Johns Hopkins University Press.

Miley, W. (1999). *The Psychology of Well Being*. Praeger Publishers.

Mitchell JE. de Zwaan M. Roerig JL. (2003). Drug therapy for patients with eating disorders. [Review] [118 refs] Current Drug Targets - CNS & Neurological Disorders. 2(1):17-29.

Mondimore, F. (2002). *Adolescent Depression: A Guide for Parents*. Baltimore: The Johns Hopkins University Press.

Natenshon, A. (1999). *When Your Child Has An Eating Disorder*. San Francisco: Jossey-Bass.

Pederson KJ. Roerig JL. Mitchell JE. (2003). Towards the pharmacotherapy of eating disorders. [Review] [160 refs] Expert Opinion on Pharmacotherapy. 4(10):1659-78.

Peterson, C & Mitchell, J. Psychosocial and Pharmacological Treatment of Eating Disorders: A Review of Research Findings. *Journal of Clinical Psychology*. Vol. 55(6)685-697 (1999)

Pettit, C. (2003). Starving: *A Personal Journey Through Anorexia*. Grand Rapids, MI: Revell.

Rio, L, and Rio, T. (2003). *The Anorexia Diaries*. PA: Rodale Press.

Schaefer, J. with Rutledge, T. (2004). *Life Without Ed*. NY: McGraw Hill.

Schneider, J.A., & Agras, W.S. (1987). Bulimia in males: A matched comparison with females. *International Journal of Eating Disorders*, 6, 235-242.

Shuman, E. Confession of a Binge Eater. *Cincinnati Magazine*, 1994.

Shiltz, T. (1997). *Eating Concerns Support Group Curriculum*. Greenfield, WI: Community Recovery Press.

Siegel, M., Brisman, J., and Weinshel, M. (1997). *Surviving an Eating Disorder: Strategies for Family and Friends*. NY: Harper Perennial.

Spitzberg, B. & Cupach, W. (1998). *The Dark Side of Close Relationships*. Lawrence Erlbaum Associates.

Teachman, B., Schwartz, M., Gordic, B., & Coyle, B. (2003). *Helping Your Child Overcome and Eating Disorder*. Oakland, CA: New Harbinger Publications.

Wertheim, E.H. *et al.* (1992). Psychosocial predictors of weight loss behaviors and binge eating in adolescent girls and boys. *International Journal of Eating Disorders*, 12, 151-160.

Wolf, N. (1991). *The Beauty Myth*. New York: William Morrow.

Zerbe, K. (1995). *The Body Betrayed: A Deeper Understanding of Women, Eating Disorders, and Treatment*. Oceanside, CA: Gurze Books.

Zerbe, K. (1999). *Women's Mental Health in Primary Care*. W.B. Saunders.

For additional information and resources,
please visit
www.starvingfamily.com